BENJAMIN'S SALE OF GOODS

SPECIAL SUPPLEMENT TO THE 6th EDITION

SALE AND SUPPLY OF GOODS TO CONSUMERS REGULATIONS 2002

AUSTRALIA
Law Book Co.
Sydney

CANADA AND USA
Carswell
Toronto

HONG KONG
Sweet & Maxwell Asia

NEW ZEALAND
Brookers
Wellington

SINGAPORE AND MALAYSIA
Sweet & Maxwell Asia
Singapore and Kuala Lumpur

Published in 2003 by Sweet and Maxwell Limited of
100 Avenue Road
London NW3 3PF
www.sweetandmaxwell.co.uk

Typeset by MFK Information Services, Stevenage, Herts.
Printed and bound in Great Britain by MPG Books

No natural forests were destroyed to make this product; only farmed timber was
used and replanted.

A CIP catalogue record for this book is available from
the British Library

ISBN 0 421 85070 1

[iv]

PREFACE

As was noted in the Preface to *Benjamin's Sale of Goods*, (6th edition), the proposed Sale and Supply of Goods to Consumers Regulations had not been made when that edition went to press. Hence it had not been possible to provide detailed commentary on them. The Regulations were eventually made on December 10, 2002 and they came into force on March 31, 2003. This special supplement has been written by some of the editors of the principal text to explain the changes introduced by what are often complex provisions.

The Regulations, which were made under section 2(2) of the European Communities Act 1972, implement, albeit belatedly, Directive 1999/44/EC of the European Parliament and of the Council on certain aspects of the sale of consumer goods and associated guarantees. They do so principally by amending primary legislation, notably, in the context of *Benjamin*, parts of the Sale of Goods Act 1979 and the Unfair Contract Terms Act 1977. For example, amendments have been made to section 14 of the 1979 Act in relation to the definition of the term "satisfactory quality" and, more controversially, to the rules on the passing of risk. These changes, which apply only where the buyer "deals as consumer" (a category of persons defined by reference to an amended section 12 of the Unfair Contract Terms Act), are relatively minor when compared to the important new remedies which are enacted in amendments introduced as a new Part 5A of the 1979 Act. Those who deal as consumers may now, in certain circumstances, call on the seller of non-conforming goods to repair or replace them or may seek a reduction in the purchase price or rescission of the contract. However, these new remedies, which are familiar in civil law systems, do not stand alone. Rather, they operate alongside the traditional common law remedies of rejection and/or claiming damages for breach of contract which are rightly retained. The interaction between the two systems may prove complex and the outcome could be difficult to predict. The Regulations also contain potentially important provisions affecting the enforceability of manufacturers' guarantees.

The text which follows explores these and related issues in some detail with frequent references to relevant sections of the principal work. However, it is intended to be a free-standing commentary which will assist readers who do not have immediate access to *Benjamin*, but who need to be in a position to give informed advice, whether to persons who deal as consumers or to sellers or other suppliers of goods.

As with the text of *Benjamin*, the commentary is a statement of the position in English law. However, the separate Regulations and provisions which apply to consumer contracts under the laws of Scotland are printed for convenience. The text of the Sale of Goods Act 1979 with amendments up to and including those introduced by the Regulations is printed as an Appendix as is the Directive on which the Regulations are based.

C. J. Miller
University of Birmingham, May 2003

CONTENTS

TABLE OF CASES

References are to paragraph numbers

TABLE OF CASES

TABLE OF STATUTES

[xi]

TABLE OF STATUTORY INSTRUMENTS

TABLE OF DECISIONS, DIRECTIVES AND REGULATIONS

TABLE OF EUROPEAN TREATIES

TABLE OF INTERNATIONAL CONVENTIONS

The Sale and Supply of Goods to Consumers Regulations 2002

(SI 2002/3045)

Made	*10th December 2002*
Laid before Parliament	*11th December 2002*
Coming into force	*31st March 2003*

The Secretary of State, being a Minister designated for the purposes of section 2(2) of the European Communities Act 1972 in relation to measures relating to consumer protection, in exercise of the powers conferred on her by that subsection, makes the following Regulations:

INTRODUCTION AND GENERAL NOTE

The Sale and Supply of Goods to Consumers Regulations 2002 (SI   **1–001** 2002/3045) were made under section 2(2) of the European Communities Act 1972 with a view to implementing Directive 1999/44/EC of the European Parliament and of the Council on certain aspects of the sale of consumer goods and associated guarantees. The general scope of the Directive and its main provisions are discussed in *Benjamin* (paras 14–017—14–029) and the Directive itself is printed below (see Appendix B). It is important to note at the outset that, although the amendments to the Sale of Goods Act 1979 introduced by Regulations 3 to 5 inclusive apply only where the buyer "deals as consumer", a business and even a company may fall within this category, provided that the purchase of the goods is not an integral part of that business or necessarily incidental thereto. The reason for this is that the expression is defined in section 61(5A) of the 1979 Act by reference to Part I of the Unfair Contract Terms Act 1977 and the relevant provision of the 1977 Act, section 12(1)(a), has been so interpreted: see *R&B Customs Brokers Ltd* v *United Dominions Trust Ltd* [1988] 1 W.L.R. 321 and, in general, *Benjamin*, para.13–071. By way of contrast, Regulation 15, which is concerned with consumer guarantees, applies only where goods are sold or otherwise supplied to a "consumer" and this category of persons is defined by the Regulations themselves (see Regulation 2, below, paras 1–054—1–057) (as opposed to the 1979 Act) to mean "any natural person who ... is acting for purposes which are outside his trade, business or profession." So, there are two distinct definitions, namely of (i) "deals as consumer" and (ii) "consumer", the former being by far the more important in the context of the Regulations as a whole.

BACKGROUND

1–002   The origins of Directive 1999/44/EC may be traced to a Council Resolution of April 14, 1975 on a preliminary programme for a consumer protection and information policy (O.J. C92/1). This refers, *inter alia*, (see para.24 (iii)) to the protection of consumers against unfair commercial practices in conditions in guarantees, particularly for consumer durables. Harmonisation of certain aspects of what were called "legal" and "commercial" guarantees (terms which are not used in the Directive) was initially linked to the issue of controlling unfair contract terms (see O.J. C243/2 and O.J. C73/7). However, the Council resolved to proceed with what was to become Directive 93/13/EEC on unfair terms in consumer contracts and to remit the wider issue of harmonising guarantee schemes to the Commission. Matters then progressed through a very wide-ranging Green Paper on Guarantees for consumer goods and after-sales services which was presented by the Commission on November 15, 1993 (COM (93) 509 final). This led to a proposal for a Directive (COM (95) 520 final), but it was more limited in scope than the Green Paper. In particular, the proposal covered only harmonisation in relation to the "legal" guarantee (broadly equivalent to the area covered by sections 13 and 14 of the Sale of Goods Act, 1979), together with associated remedies for its breach, and the "commercial" guarantee typically offered by manufacturers of goods. As was noted in the accompanying Explanatory Memorandum, the issue of after-sales service linked to the maintenance and repair of goods was not included since it was seen as being better suited to regulation at a national level. The Commission commented that after-sales service was "a complex domain which is more adequately addressed, at Community level, through voluntary instruments (for example codes of conduct for individual sectors) than in the form of statutory rules." The proposal was subjected to incisive scrutiny in the *Report of the House of Lords Select Committee on the European Communities, Consumer Guarantees* (1996–97 HL 57) and to much comment elsewhere (see, for example, Bradgate [1995] Consum. L.J. 94 and Beale and Howells 12 J.C.L. 21 (1997)). The text of the Directive which was eventually adopted and which entered into force on July 7, 1999 differs in a number of respects from earlier proposals.

THE LEGAL BASIS OF THE DIRECTIVE

Directive 1999/44/EC was adopted pursuant to Article 95 of the   **1-003**
Treaty [formerly Article 100a] and hence on the basis that its object
was to improve the conditions for the establishment and functioning
of the internal market. Article 95.3 requires that proposals for achieving harmonisation in the area, *inter alia*, of consumer protection must
take as their base a high level of protection. This is supported by
Article 153.1 of the Treaty [formerly Article 129a] which contains a
Community obligation to contribute to protecting the health, safety
and economic interests of consumers in order to ensure a high level of
consumer protection. The European Court of Justice has recently
examined Article 95 in considerable detail in the context of upholding
the validity of Directive 2001/37 EC (The Tobacco Directive): see *R. v
Secretary of State for Health*; *Ex p. British American Tobacco (Invest-
ments) Ltd* (Case C–491/01) [2003] 1 C.M.L.R. 14. In the case of
Directive 1999/44/EC the Explanatory Memorandum to which reference was made above asserts that the measures would have the following benefits, namely: "strengthen consumer confidence in the
single market; facilitate cross-border shopping and strengthen the
role of consumers as active market players; simplify existing national
rules; bring Community law closer to European citizens by giving
them direct and very tangible benefits. Hence strengthen the Community citizen's support for European integration; have positive
effects on competition, business competitiveness and the European
economy." The facilitation of cross-border shopping and the removal
of distortions to competition are also referred to in the preamble to
the Directive. Clearly it can be argued that there are many more practical barriers to cross-border shopping—access to justice, the territorial limits of guarantees, the obvious difficulty of returning bulky
goods to some far-distant place of purchase, etc.—but the legal validity of the Directive appears to be secure and it is, in any event, most
unlikely to be challenged.

MINIMUM PROTECTION

It is important to note that Directive 1999/44/EC provides for only a   **1-004**
minimum level of protection, Article 8.1 states that: "The rights
resulting from this Directive shall be exercised without prejudice to
other rights which the consumer may invoke under the national rules
governing contractual or non-contractual liability." Article 8.2 in turn
provides that: "Member States may adopt or maintain in force more
stringent provisions, compatible with the Treaty in the field covered
by this Directive, to ensure a higher level of consumer protection." In
this it is to be contrasted with Council Directive 85/374/EEC (the

Product Liability Directive) which (subject to the provisions of Article 13 and the limited areas where derogation is possible) has been held to be a maximum Directive setting out rights which cannot be exceeded in order to provide a higher level of consumer protection: (see *Benjamin*, para.14–074) and Case C–52/00 *Commission of the European Communities* v *French Republic*; Case C–154/00 *Commission of the European Communities* v *Hellenic Republic*; Case C–183/00 *Sanchez* v *Medicina Asturiana SA* (ECJ, April 25, 2002). It will be seen (below, paras 1–015—1–023, 1–105 *et seq.*) that the relationship between the existing remedies of the Sale of Goods Act 1979 (see *Benjamin*, paras 12–017—12–070, 17–046 *et seq.*) and the additional remedies afforded by Regulation 5 and the new Part 5A of the Act to those who deal as consumers is by no means straightforward. Certainly, it does not support the claim in the Explanatory Memorandum noted above that the Directive will "simplify existing national rules". On the contrary, it has, at least for the purposes of English law, made them much more complex.

IMPLEMENTATION OF THE DIRECTIVE

1–005 The process of implementing Directive 1999/44/EC proved to be a lengthy one. The Department of Trade and Industry issued a First Consultation Paper (URN 00/1471) on January 4, 2001, but this revealed such considerable underlying difficulties that it was necessary to issue a Second Consultation Paper with accompanying draft Regulations (URN 02/538) on February 26, 2002. The delay was partly attributable to a decision to implement the Directive by amending primary legislation (principally, although not solely, the Sale of Goods Act 1979), rather than by simply copying it out in free-standing Regulations. This method has obvious advantages in that it avoids the problems associated with the separate but overlapping provisions currently found in the Unfair Contract Terms Act 1977 and the Unfair Terms in Consumer Contracts Regulations 1999, (SI 1999/2083), as amended (see *Benjamin*, paras 13–062—13–096, 14–030—14–041). However, it has to be said that some of the amendments, notably those associated with the new Part 5A of the 1979 Act, do not sit easily within the framework of the Act as a whole. Indeed, they may be seen as providing support for the argument that the time has come to introduce separate legislation covering consumer sales, including exemption clauses and potentially unfair contract terms. (see M. Bridge, (2003) 119 L.Q.R. 173). The possible effect of non-implementation by the prescribed date, January 1, 2002, is referred to in the note to Regulation 1, below.

SUMMARY OF THE MAIN PROVISIONS

The main provisions of the Regulations are commented on in some   **1–006**
detail in the pages which follow. This introductory note contains a
brief summary. Regulation 1 provides, *inter alia,* for the Regulations
to come into force on March 31, 2003, and Regulation 2 contains
interpretative provisions defining such words as "consumer" and
"guarantee".

*Amendment of section 14 (implied condition as to satisfactory
quality)*

Regulation 3 is included for the purpose of implementing that part of   **1–007**
Article 2 of the Directive (namely Article 2.2(d) and 2.4) which may
not already have been covered by the combined scope of sections 13
and 14 of the Sale of Goods Act 1979. In particular, section 14(2D) is
inserted to add further designated circumstances which may be relevant for the purposes of section 14(2A) when determining whether
goods are of satisfactory quality so as to meet the requirement of section 14(2) of the Act (see, generally, *Benjamin*, paras 11–026 *et seq.*).
So, subject to the qualifications of the new section 14(2E), the relevant
circumstances include "any public statements on the specific characteristics of the goods made about them by the seller, the producer [as
defined in Regulation 6, amending section 61(1)] or his representative, particularly in advertising or on labelling." Such public statements might be made, for example, on the television or radio, in the
press or on hoardings, at the point of sale, or on labels or in
accompanying literature. Equivalent changes are made in related
legislation, notably by Regulations 7 and 10 which amend sections 4
and 9 of the Supply of Goods and Services Act 1982 (covering,
respectively, contracts for work and materials, etc. and for the hire of
goods) and by Regulation 13 which amends section 10 of the Supply of
Goods (Implied Terms) Act 1973 (contracts of hire-purchase).

The new section 14(2D) is applicable only where the buyer deals as   **1–008**
consumer, but, as section 14(2F) makes clear, its substance, including
the qualifications of section 14(2E), may be of more general application and be potentially applicable in commercial transactions as
well. Statements about the characteristics of the goods which are
descriptive and on labels accompanying the goods already typically
fall within the implied condition of correspondence with description
of section 13 of the 1979 Act, which of course applies irrespective of
whether the buyer deals as consumer (see *Benjamin*, paras 11–001 *et*

seq.). Section 14(2F) points to the possibility that public statements made in advertising or on labelling, etc. may, on appropriate facts, be similarly relevant to the issue of satisfactory quality under section 14(2) of the Act.

1–009 Finally, it should be noted that the context of Regulation 3 and the new section 14(2D) is, of course, the liability of the seller. The amendment does not address the distinct issue of a manufacturer's potential liability for non-compliance with claims made in advertising or other public statements. This basis of liability, sometimes referred to as the express warranty theory, has been developed elsewhere, notably in the USA (see *Benjamin*, para.14–072).

Contracts for work and materials: incorrect installation

1–010 There has been some discussion about the meaning of Article 1.4 which provides that: "Contracts for the supply of consumer goods to be manufactured or produced shall also be deemed contracts of sale for the purpose of this Directive." The French version is similarly worded and refers to "contrats de fourniture de biens de consommation à fabriquer ou à produire". On one interpretation this does no more than make it clear that the Directive covers what in English law would be called contracts for the sale of "future goods" (see section 5(2) of the Sale of Goods Act, 1979). An alternative interpretation is that it extends the Directive to cover the production and supply of such custom-made or bespoke items as suits, furniture and presumably even portraits. This is the interpretation favoured in the Department of Trade and Industry Consultation Papers to which reference was made above (see para.1–005). In English law such contracts would usually be described as contracts for work and materials, rather than of sale (see, generally, *Benjamin*, paras 1–041—1–042). Again, it might be suggested that if such contracts are deemed to be contracts of sale for the purpose of the Directive it would be strange if the same were not similarly true of other contracts for work and materials in which the goods were not "manufactured or produced" to special order. Examples of such contracts might include contracts to repair a car, using a standard replacement part, or to roof a house.

1–011 It is submitted that on balance the wording of Article 1.4 points to its being interpreted in line with the first alternative mooted above, that is, of making it clear that "future" goods are covered, but no more. However, Regulations 7 and 9 go well beyond this and extend both the additional factors to be taken into account in determining whether goods are of satisfactory quality and, more importantly, the new remedies to all contracts within the scope of Part I of the Supply of Goods and Services Act 1982, including contracts for work and materials. So, contracts to repair a car using a standard replacement part would be subject to the new provisions. There are no equivalent changes in the 1982 Act to those introduced into the Sale of Goods Act by Regulation 4 (passing of risk and acceptance of goods). However, as is explained below (see para.1–077) it is at best doubtful whether the changes introduced by Regulation 4 were necessary in order to comply with the Directive. In any event, it is clear that Article 1.4 does not necessitate extensive assimilation of the law which applies to contracts for the sale of goods and contracts for work and materials. Even on the most extended meaning which might be attributed to it, it applies only "for the purpose of this Directive" and this purpose is a relatively narrow one.

The requirement as to conformity with the contract of Article 2 of the   **1–012**
Directive contains a further provision in Article 2.5 which states that: "Any lack of conformity resulting from incorrect installation of the consumer goods shall be deemed to be equivalent to lack of conformity of the goods if installation forms part of the contract of sale of the goods and the goods were installed by the seller or under his responsibility. This shall apply equally if the product, intended to be installed by the consumer, is installed by the consumer and the incorrect installation is due to a shortcoming in the installation instructions."

The first part of this provision is concerned with what English law   **1–013**
would refer to as contracts for work and materials (see above) and the relevant implementing provision is Regulation 9, which inserts a new section 11S into the Supply of Goods and Services Act 1982 to define when goods are not in conformity with the contract. Section 11S(1)(b) refers to an installation by the transferor, or under his responsibility, "in breach of the term implied by section 13" of the 1982 Act, that is, of an obligation to carry out the service with reasonable care and skill. However, as is noted below (see paras 1–190, 1–241), it is doubtful whether Article 2.5 envisages only a negligence-based, as opposed to a strict, liability, and hence it is probable that the Directive has not been correctly implemented in this respect. Stricter obligations have been recognised in other contexts and in order to give effect to the intentions of the parties (see, for example, *Greaves & Co (Contractors) Ltd* v *Baynham Meikle and Partners* [1975] 1 W.L.R. 1095, which involved a building contract) and this possibility is preserved by section 16(3)(a) of the 1982 Act which confirms that an obligation stricter than that imposed by section 13 may exist on appropriate facts. However, the explicit reference to section 13 in the new section 11S(1)(b) makes it difficult to argue that resort may be had to section

16(3)(a) so as to give effect to Article 2.5. The second part of Article 2.5, which concerns shortcomings in installation instructions, is already covered under the general provisions as to satisfactory quality of section 14(2) of the 1979 Act and section 4(2) of the 1982 Act (see *Benjamin*, para.11–051 and sources there cited). However, it may give rise to considerable difficulty in connection with the possible application of the new Part 5A remedies which are discussed below (see paras 1–105 *et seq.*).

Passing of risk and acceptance of goods

1–014   Regulation 4 amends sections 20 and 32 of the 1979 Act in cases where the buyer deals as consumer. By Regulation 4(2) a new section 20(4) is inserted into the 1979 Act thereby displacing the general rules of section 20(1) to (3) of the Act, including the presumption that when property in goods is transferred to the buyer the goods are at the buyer's risk whether delivery has been made or not (see *Benjamin*, para.5–016). Section 20(4) now provides that where the buyer deals as consumer the goods will remain at the seller's risk until they are delivered to the consumer. Regulation 4(3) inserts a new section 32(4) into the 1979 Act so that where the buyer deals as consumer one must ignore the presumption that a required or authorised delivery to a carrier for the purpose of transmission to the buyer is to be treated as delivery to the buyer (see *Benjamin*, para.8–014). The new section 32(4) states that in such cases "delivery of goods to the carrier is not delivery of the goods to the buyer." In general terms the combined effect is that the risk of loss of or damage to the goods during transit will remain with the seller. Regulation 4 is linked to Article 2.2 of the Directive, which requires the seller to "deliver goods to the consumer which are in conformity with the contract of sale" and Article 3.1 which makes the seller liable for any lack of conformity which exists at the time the goods were delivered. However, as is explained below (see para.1–077) the new provisions go significantly beyond that which was needed to implement the requirements of the Directive.

The new Part 5A remedies

1–015   If the above changes are for the most part relatively modest in scope, the same cannot be said of Regulation 5, which adds a new Part 5A (sections 48A to 48F) to the 1979 Act. This corresponds to Article 3 of the Directive and it provides an important and complex set of additional remedies to a buyer who deals as consumer. The general scheme of Part 5A is to create what may be seen as a hierarchy of remedies which are available to such buyers when the goods fail to conform to the contract at the time of delivery through breach of an express term of the contract or a term implied by sections 13, 14 or 15 of the Act (see section 48F).

In applying these provisions the new section 48A(3) implements   **1–016**
Article 5.3 of the Directive by enacting a potentially important presumption of non-conformity operative over a period of six months starting with the date on which the goods were delivered to the buyer. For the purpose of the Part 5A remedies, any non-conformity which becomes apparent within six months of delivery is to be presumed to have existed at the date of delivery. The presumption is rebuttable in the sense that the seller may establish that the goods did so conform at the date of delivery and it will not in any event apply if it is incompatible with the nature of the goods or the nature of the lack of conformity (section 48A(4)).

Assuming that the goods do not conform to the contract of sale at the   **1–017**
time of delivery, the buyer who deals as consumer may require the seller to repair or replace them and to effect this "cure" within a reasonable time and without causing significant inconvenience to the buyer (sections 48A(2)(a) and 48B(1) and (2)(a)). These matters are to be determined by reference to the nature of the goods and the purpose for which they were acquired (section 48B(5)). The initial choice as between "repair" (defined by section 61(1) of the Act, as inserted by Regulation 6(2), to mean "to bring the goods into conformity with the contract") and "replacement" appears to lie with the buyer. In both cases the seller must bear any necessary costs, including in particular the costs of any labour, materials or postage (section 48B(2)(b)).

However, section 48B(3) places restrictions on the entitlement of a   **1–018**
buyer to require that non-conforming goods be repaired or, as the case may be, replaced. In particular, the remedies must not be required if they are (a) impossible or (b) disproportionate, whether in comparison to each other or in comparison to the remedies of a reduction of the purchase price or rescission to which reference is made below. For example, repair may sometimes be impossible when the non-conformity takes the form of a breach of section 13 of the Act, as by delivering goods which are of the wrong colour, size or make. Replacement may be similarly impossible in the case of second-hand goods (an example given in para.(16) of the preamble to the Directive) and no doubt in other cases where goods have some unique or even special quality. The test of whether a given remedy is disproportionate is primarily judged by reference to the costs which are imposed on the seller (section 48B(4)), although account is also taken

of whether an alternative remedy could be effected without significant inconvenience to the buyer.

1–019   In support of these remedies, section 48E(2) empowers a court to make an order requiring specific performance of an obligation to repair or, as the case may be, replace the goods. This complements the established power under section 52 of the Act to require the seller to deliver the contract goods, rather than retain them and pay damages (see, generally, *Benjamin*, paras 17–094 *et seq.*). It would be moderately surprising if this new remedy came to be used other than in exceptional cases, especially in the case of repair, where there would be scope for dispute as to whether the goods had been brought into conformity with the contract. In many (and probably most) cases, it is likely that a court will fall back on an alternative Part 5A remedy which it considers to be more appropriate.

1–020   Section 48C(1) of the Act makes provision for what appear to be seen as secondary or second-tier remedies, namely a reduction in the purchase price (a novel remedy in English law) or rescission of the contract. However, these remedies are not available unless the conditions of section 48C(2) are satisfied. In essence, repair and replacement must be impossible or disproportionate and so cannot be required or, if they are available in principle, the seller must have failed to comply with section 48(B)(2)(a) by repairing or, as the case may be, replacing the goods within a reasonable time and without significant inconvenience to the buyer. If the buyer rescinds the contract then by sections 48C(3) and 48E(5) the reimbursement to him of the purchase price may be reduced to take account of the use he had had of the non-conforming goods since they were delivered to him. The new Part 5A does not contain a direct equivalent of Article 3.6 of the Directive, which provides that: "The consumer is not entitled to have the contract rescinded if the lack of conformity is minor." However, as already noted (above, para.1–004), the Directive sets only minimum requirements and the established remedies will continue to apply, for example, as for a breach of section 13 of the 1979 Act, unless the *de minimis* principle is applicable (see, generally, *Benjamin*, para.11–018).

1–021   Section 48D implicitly recognises the continued existence of the traditional remedies of the common law and of the Sale of Goods Act. These are discussed in detail in *Benjamin* (see, especially, Chs 12, 14–014—14–016 and 17) and a buyer who deals as consumer may continue to rely on them. In brief, he may reject the goods and/or terminate the contract for breach (see *Benjamin*, paras 12–017 *et seq.*), although these remedies will be lost, usually within a relatively short period of time (although see in this connection *Clegg* v *Andersson* [2003] EWCA Civ 320, [2003] 2 Lloyd's Rep. 32), by acceptance of the goods under section 35 of the 1979 Act (see *Benjamin*, paras 12–044 *et seq.*). The existing remedy of diminution or extinction of the price for breach of warranty of quality conferred by section 53(1) of the 1979 Act (see *Benjamin*, para.17–048) is also left intact to operate side by side with the new remedy of a reduction of the price under section 48C(1)(a).

The Regulations make little attempt to assist buyers who deal as con-   **1–022**
sumers to navigate between these two sets of remedies. In fact, the only relevant provision is to be found in the new section 48D of the Act. This provides that if a buyer has required a seller to repair or replace the goods he must give him a reasonable time in which to do so. In particular, he must not in the meantime purport to reject the goods and terminate the contract for breach of condition, nor require the goods to be replaced when previously he had required them to be repaired, or *vice-versa*. Presumably, the sense is that any such action, if taken prematurely, will be legally ineffective. Critical issues such as switching remedies between the established and the new Part 5A provisions and the relationship between repair and replacement and the loss of the right to reject through acceptance are discussed further in the notes to sections 48A to 48F, below.

Finally, in this context it should be noted that provisions which are   **1–023**
equivalent to Part 5A of the 1979 Act are added as a new Part 1B (sections 11M to 11S) to the Supply of Goods and Services Act 1982 to confer additional rights on transferees who deal as consumers. This covers cases involving contracts for the transfer of property in goods within section 1 of that Act (contracts for work and materials, etc.), but not contracts of hire-purchase or of hire. The nature of contracts for work and materials is, however, such that a remedy of replacement of non-conforming goods may more readily be judged disproportionate.

The definition of 'deals as consumer'

Regulation 14 amends section 12 of the Unfair Contract Terms Act   **1–024**
1977 and hence the Sale of Goods Act definition of a person who "deals as consumer". The immediate effect of this is to draw a distinction according to whether or not the person claiming to deal as consumer is an individual. Where he is an individual section 12(1)(c) does not apply and so, for a buyer to deal as consumer, the goods no longer have to be "of a type ordinarily supplied for private use or consump-

tion." This is in line with the definition of "consumer" and "consumer goods" in Article 1.2 of the Directive, the latter definition being very broad and not limited by a requirement similar to that of section 12(1)(c). Conversely, section 12(1)(c) will continue to apply where the buyer is, for example, a company which may still, in principle, deal as consumer if the goods are not bought as an integral part of the business or as something necessarily incidental to it (see, generally, *R&B Customs Brokers Co Ltd* v *United Dominions Trust Ltd* [1988] 1 W.L.R. 321; *Benjamin*, para.13–071).

1–025   The substitution of section 12(2) of the 1977 Act, setting out further circumstances in which buyers are not to be regarded as dealing as consumers, again draws the same distinction between individuals and others. The new section 12(2)(a) mirrors and takes advantage of Article 1.3 of the Directive which states that: "Member States may provide that the expression 'consumer goods' does not cover second-hand goods sold at public auction where consumers have the opportunity of attending the sale in person." This does not cover other auction sales and sales by competitive tender where, contrary to the superseded version of section 12(2), individuals will deal as consumer, provided that the requirements of section 12(1) are met. Those who are not individuals will, as before, not deal as consumers where the relevant sale is by an auction of whatever kind or by competitive tender. The overall picture is now one of considerable complexity and is commented on further in the notes to Regulation 14 (see below, paras 1–250 *et seq.*).

1–026   As already noted (see para.1–001), the importance of the above provisions extends beyond the immediate context of the Unfair Contract Terms Act 1977, which includes (but is not limited to) the question of whether buyers receive complete protection against terms which seek to exclude or restrict liability for breach of the conditions implied by sections 13, 14 and 15 of the 1979 Act. The amendments introduced by Regulations 3 to 5 inclusive apply only where the buyer "deals as consumer" and this expression is defined in section 61(5A) of the Sale of Goods Act by reference to Part I (section 12) of the Unfair Contract Terms Act.

Consumer guarantees

1–027   Regulation 15, which is concerned with consumer guarantees (see Regulation 2, below), corresponds to Article 6 of the Directive (see *Benjamin*, paras 14–062 *et seq.*). Neither requires manufacturers or sellers to provide such guarantees, although they are commonly to be found in such areas as the sale of electrical goods and motor cars. The purpose, rather, is to provide that any such guarantee shall take effect as a contractual obligation and, as such, be binding on the guarantor. Additional requirements of form and content are also prescribed: in particular the guarantee must be in plain and intelligible language and in English. Powers are given to enforcement authorities to apply for an injunction to secure compliance with Regulation 15.

PROVISIONS NOT DIRECTLY OR FULLY IMPLEMENTED

There are several provisions in Directive 1999/44/EC which do not have an equivalent in the Regulations.   **1–028**

Article 2.3

Article 2.3 is concerned with two situations in which there shall be   **1–029**
deemed not to be a lack of conformity of the goods with the contract of sale. The extent to which this corresponds with the position under section 14 of the Sale of Goods Act 1979 is considered below (see paras 1–071—1–074) when commenting on the changes introduced by Regulation 3.

Article 4

Article 4 is concerned with the right of redress which a final or retail   **1–030**
seller may have when held liable to a consumer for the non-conformity of the goods. Such issues are left to be determined by national law and in English law they would be covered by the usual chain of liability whereby the retailer would typically sue his wholesale seller who would in turn sue the manufacturer who sold the goods to him.

Article 5

Article 5 contains two time limits, other than the six month presump-   **1–031**
tion of Article 5.3 to which reference has already been made (see above, para.1–016; also, below, paras 1–108—1–112). One such limit in Article 5.2 permits Member States to require consumers to inform the seller of the lack of conformity within a period of two months from the date on which they detected it. There is no such requirement in English law and it has not been introduced in this context. The second time limit is that of Article 5.1 which states that: "The seller shall be held liable under Article 3 where the lack of conformity becomes apparent within two years as from delivery of the goods. If, under national legislation, the rights laid down in Article 3.1 are subject to a limitation period, that period shall not expire within a period of two years from the time of delivery." By Article 7.1 a shorter time limit of not less than one year may be introduced in the case of second-hand

goods. The rights of Article 3.2 are those of repair, replacement, a reduction in the price or rescission of the contract.

1–032   The implications of this provision in the context of a Directive which establishes minimum levels of protection are noted below (at paras 1–214—1–215). Here it is sufficient to observe that, if called upon to do so, the buyer must still establish (albeit, with the benefit where applicable of the six month presumption of the new section 48A(3)) (see below, paras 1–108—1–112) that the goods did not conform to the contract on delivery (see *Benjamin*, para.11–052). As for the reference to a minimum two year limitation period, this was not taken up and English law exceeds this by a considerable margin since the relevant period prescribed by the Limitation Act 1980 in a claim for breach of contract is six years.

Article 7.1 and 7.2

1–033   Finally, the Regulations do not contain an equivalent of Article 7.1 and 7.2 of the Directive which establishes its binding nature. The first part of Article 7.1 (inability as provided for by national law to waive or restrict rights resulting from the Directive) is, in effect, covered by sections 6(2) and 7(2) of the Unfair Contract Terms Act 1977 which, in cases where the buyer or transferee deals as consumer (see above, paras 1–024—1–026 and below, paras 1–250 *et seq.*) render ineffective any attempt to exclude or restrict liability for breach of the implied conditions of sections 13 to 15 of the 1979 Act. Section 13 of the 1977 Act defines the notion of "excluding or restricting" liability broadly so as to cover the curtailing of rights or remedies (see *Benjamin*, paras 13–064 *et seq.*).

Article 12

1–034   Article 12 is also of general interest in requiring the Commission to report on the application of the Directive not later than July 7, 2006. It also stipulates that the report shall examine the case for introducing what it refers to as "the producer's direct liability" and, if appropriate, shall be accompanied by proposals. Any such liability would, in effect, subject manufacturers to a direct and strict liability to consumers with whom they have no contractual relationship and the liability would presumably extend to instances where the only loss was financial or economic. There are examples of such an extended liability in other common law jurisdictions, but it would represent a major change in English law. Moreover, it would be incompatible with the provisions of Part I of the Consumer Protection Act 1987 and Council Directive 85/374/EEC on liability for defective products, both of which limit the liability of producers to cases of death, personal injury and, broadly speaking, damage to consumer-type property.

ANTI-AVOIDANCE ISSUES

Article 7.2 of the Directive contains an anti-avoidance provision. **1–035** "Member States shall take the necessary measures to ensure that consumers are not deprived of the protection afforded by this Directive as the result of opting for the law of a non-member State as the law applicable to the contract where the contract has a close connection with the territory of the Member States". In terms, this provision is very similar to, but not identical with, equivalent provisions in Council Directive 1993/13/EEC on unfair terms in consumer contracts (Article 6.2) and Directive 1997/7/EC of the European Parliament and of the Council on the protection of consumers in respect of distance contracts (Article 10.2): see *Benjamin*, paras 25–101, 25–107, 25–111. Each of these provisions was transposed directly into the Regulations by which these Directives were implemented: see, respectively, Unfair Terms in Consumer Contracts Regulations 1999 (SI 1999/2083, as amended by SI 2001/1186), Regulation 9; Consumer Protection (Distance Selling) Regulations 2000 (SI 2000/2334), Regulation 25(2), discussed in *Benjamin*, paras 25–10—25–110. In contrast, Article 7.2 has not been so transposed into the present Regulations.

The reason for this is, apparently, that it is thought that the obligation **1–036** to transpose Article 7.2 is discharged in existing legislation, namely section 27 of the Unfair Contract Terms Act 1977: see Department of Trade and Industry, Consumer and Competition Policy Directorate, *Directive 1999/44/EC of the European Parliament and of the Council of May 25, 1999 on certain aspects of the sale of consumer goods and associated guarantees, Transposition Note*. As stated above (see para.1–033), sections 6(2) and 7(2) of this Act, together with section 13, prevent direct or indirect exclusion or restriction against persons dealing as consumer of the seller's duties as laid down in ss.13 to 15 of the Sale of Goods Act (see *Benjamin*, paras 13–064—13–066, 13–076, 13–077); and as regards sale of goods it is on these sections of the Sale of Goods Act that the Regulations mostly operate. (The matter is further discussed in connection with the new Part 5A: see below, paras 1–219—1–221). It seems to have been assumed therefore that so long as the Unfair Contract Terms Act itself could not be avoided by a choice of law, the provisions of the Regulations could not either.

This assumption may not in fact be entirely correct. The effect of **1–037** Regulation 4, which amends the Sale of Goods Act rules as to delivery, largely relates to risk and can only doubtfully be said to involve direct or indirect exclusion of the quality duties laid down by sections 13 to 15 of the Sale of Goods Act. The provisions as to consumer guarantees in Regulation 15 are clearly freestanding and unrelated to sections 13 to 15. These are slight matters, in particular because Regulation 15 does not require the giving of guarantees, but simply applies if a guarantee is given. More serious however is that section 27 of the Unfair Contract Terms Act itself may not in this context always have the effect and coverage assumed, as will be seen from the following comments.

1–038   The anti-avoidance provision in section 27 of the Unfair Contract Terms Act 1977 is to be found in section 27(2) which provides as follows:

> "This Act has effect notwithstanding any contract term which applies or purports to apply the law of some country outside the United Kingdom, where (either or both)—
>
> (a) the term appears to the court or arbitrator or arbiter to have been imposed wholly or mainly for the purpose of enabling the party imposing it to evade the operation of this Act; or
> (b) in the making of the contract one of the parties dealt as consumer, and he was then habitually resident in the United Kingdom, and the essential steps necessary for the making of the contract were taken there, whether by him or others on his behalf."

1–039   The effect of this subsection is discussed in detail in *Benjamin*, paras 25–094—25–100, 25–152—25–153, 25–164—25–165. The following points require specific mention in the context of the present Regulations.

1–040   The principal difficulty in implementing Article 7.2 of the Directive through the Unfair Contract Terms Act 1977 lies in the fact that that Act does not apply at all where the contract is an "international supply contract", as defined in section 26 of the 1977 Act, and a contract may be an "international supply contract" for these purposes even if it is concluded by a buyer who deals as consumer. For detailed discussion of section 26 see *Benjamin*, paras 18–246, 25–090, 25–153, 25–164. It is highly likely that a cross-border contract concluded by a buyer who deals as a consumer will be excluded from the 1977 Act by section 26, as for example, in a case where a consumer habitually resident in England orders goods from a seller whose place of business is in France, it being agreed that the goods will be carried from France to England: see section 26(3) and (4); *Benjamin*, paras 18–246, 25–090. If this is correct then if the contract is expressed to be governed by French law and contains a term which purports to exclude section 14 of the Sale of Goods Act 1979, as amended by the present Regulations, then the effect of that term will be determined by French law, including the Directive as implemented in France and the controls in the 1977 Act will not apply. If the contract is expressed to be governed by English law then the validity of the exclusionary term would also have to be determined, as a result of section 26, without regard to the controls contained in the 1977 Act. And if the contract is expressed to be governed by the law of a non-member State, say the law of New York, and the exclusion of the seller's liability was effective under that law, section 26 would again seem to indicate that the controls in the 1977 Act will not apply. The outcomes in the last two examples hardly seem consistent with proper implementation of the Directive and the outcome in the third example would appear to be in direct contravention of Article 7.2 of the Directive, so that in consequence the Directive will not, in this respect, have been properly implemented in the United Kingdom.

It is unlikely, because of section 26, that section 14 of the Sale of **1–041** Goods Act 1979, as amended, or other relevant provisions of the Regulations can be construed as mandatory rules of the law of the forum applicable by virtue of Article 7.2 of the Rome Convention on the Law Applicable to Contractual Obligations, implemented in the United Kingdom in the Contracts (Applicable Law) Act 1990 (*Benjamin*, paras 25–055, 25–099) or, for the same reason, as mandatory rules of the law of the consumer's habitual residence applicable under Article 5 of the Rome Convention (*Benjamin*, paras 25–044—25–056, 25–099). It is, however, possible that a term excluding relevant provisions of the Regulations in a contract expressed to be governed by the law of a non-member State which would regard the exclusion as effective will fall foul of the Unfair Terms in Consumer Contracts Regulations 1999: see Regulations 5–8 (above, *Benjamin*, paras 14–032—14–040). Those Regulations do not contain any provision equivalent to section 26 of the Unfair Contract Terms Act 1977. Accordingly, those Regulations will apply notwithstanding the choice of the law of a non-member State if the contract has a close connection with the territory of the Member States: see Regulation 9; *Benjamin*, para.25–103. Thus, in the example given above, where the contract between the consumer and the seller contains a choice of New York law, the 1999 Regulations could, in an appropriate case, be invoked to strike down the exclusionary term.

Even if it can be established that the relevant contract is not excluded **1–042** from the Unfair Contract Terms Act 1977 by section 26 of the Act, that does not resolve the difficulties that arise, since the application of the anti-avoidance provision in section 27(2) of the 1977 Act referred to above also presents problems.

[17]

1–043 First, the opening words of the subsection stipulate that the controls in the 1977 Act apply notwithstanding any contract term which applies or purports to apply *the law of some country outside the United Kingdom*. The italicised words clearly include the laws of countries which are not Member States, as envisaged by Article 7.2 of the Directive. Thus, for example, it will not be possible, as against a buyer who deals as consumer, to exclude section 14 of the Sale of Goods Act 1979, as amended by the Regulations, by the choice of the law of a non-member State which has provisions less protective of the consumer than those which are contained in section 14, if the circumstances required by section 27(2) are present. Further, it would not, it is suggested, be possible to exclude the new remedies established by the Regulations or the provisions of the Regulations concerned with consumer guarantees by such a device. The provisions would thus apply in relation to a purchase of goods by a buyer dealing as consumer who is habitually resident in England from the English branch of a New York firm, where the goods are in England at all material times and the contract is wholly made in England, but the contract is expressed to be governed by New York law: *Cf.* Unfair Contract Terms Act 1977, sections 5, 6(2)(a) and 13(1)(b); and see *Benjamin*, paras 25–098, 25–189—25–194; as to the new section 20(4), concerned with risk, see below, para.1–093.

1–044 It will, however, be noticed that the italicised words set out above are also apt to include the laws of countries which are Member States. A literal reading of the words appears to envisage the application of the controls in the 1977 Act even where the chosen law is the law of another Member State and even where that chosen law is more favourable to the consumer (which is clearly possible since the Directive only establishes a minimum standard of protection for consumers, above, para.1–004) than are the provisions of the 1977 Act. On this basis, where a buyer dealing as consumer who is habitually resident in England purchases goods from the English branch of a French firm, where the goods are in England at all material times and the contract is wholly made in England, but the contract is expressed to be governed by French law, then the controls in the 1977 Act must be applied even if the buyer would receive greater protection under French law than he would receive under the 1977 Act. It is, however, arguable that the clear implication to be derived from Article 7.2 of the Directive is that where the contract is governed by the law of another Member State, by reason of a choice by the parties, then that State's law will be the governing law: see *Benjamin*, paras 25–102, 25–108, discussing Unfair Terms in Consumer Contracts Regulations 1999, Regulation 9 and Consumer Protection (Distance Selling) Regulations 2000, Regulation 25(5). Accordingly, it may be that the Directive envisages that the Directive, as implemented in the other Member State, should apply in such a case.

Secondly, section 27(2) of the 1977 Act can only be applied if its terms **1–045** are satisfied. It is possible, however, that a contract containing a choice of the law of a non-member State may have a close connection with England for the purposes of Article 7.2 of the Directive even though the precise requirements of section 27(2) do not exist in the particular case. Such a situation may exist where a buyer dealing as consumer is habitually resident in, for example, Germany and purchases goods from the English branch of a New York firm, where the goods are in England at all material times and the contract is wholly made in England, but the contract is expressed to be governed by the law of New York. Section 27(2)(b) cannot apply since the consumer is not habitually resident in England and it may not be possible to prove that the requirements of section 27(2)(a) are satisfied (see *Benjamin*, para.25–098) so that section 27(2) as a whole is inapplicable.

It is highly unlikely that in such circumstances relevant provisions of **1–046** the Regulations may be applicable as mandatory rules of the law of the forum pursuant to Article 7.2 of the Rome Convention on the Law Applicable to Contractual Obligations, implemented in the United Kingdom by the Contracts (Applicable Law) Act 1990: see *Benjamin*, paras 25–055, 25–099. This is because section 27(2) determines the circumstances in which those provisions will be regarded as mandatory. For the same reason it is highly unlikely that the application of Article 5 of the Rome Convention may have the effect of making relevant provisions of the Regulations applicable: see *Benjamin*, paras 25–044—25–056, 25–099. It may, however, be possible to resort to the Unfair Terms in Consumer Contracts Regulations 1999, which is not subject to the specific restrictions found in section 27(2): see *Benjamin*, para.25–103.

Thirdly, even if the terms of section 27(2) are satisfied that subsection **1–047** can only ensure the application of English law. It is possible, however, that a contract containing the choice of the law of a non-member State will have a close connection with the territory of a Member State other than the United Kingdom, though the case is brought before an English court because the seller is subject to English jurisdiction. In such a case, Article 7.2 of the Directive would seem to envisage application of the law of the Member State (including the Directive as implemented in that State) with which the contract has a close connection, but section 27(2) cannot be used to reach this conclusion.

Fourthly, reference to "section 27" of the Unfair Contract Terms Act **1–048** 1977 in the Transposition Note referred to above, para.1–036, suggests that the applicability of the controls in the 1977 Act may also depend on section 27(1) of the 1977 Act. That subsection provides that "Where the law applicable to a contract is the law of any part of the United Kingdom only by choice of the parties (and apart from that choice would be the law of some country outside the United Kingdom) sections 2 to 7 … of this Act do not operate as part of the law applicable to the contract." The provision is discussed in detail in *Benjamin*, paras 25–091—25–093.

1–049   Section 27(1) is not an anti-avoidance provision in the sense of Article 7.2 of the Directive and there is no other provision of the Directive which is equivalent to it. It would, therefore, not seem necessary to apply section 27(1) of the 1977 Act in order to comply with the Directive. Indeed, it can be said that in some circumstances application of section 27(1) can be positively inimical to the purposes of the Directive. If the provision is applicable in the present context, the effect will be that if English law is applicable only by choice of the parties, that will not prevent the exclusion of, say, section 14 of the Sale of Goods Act 1979, as amended by the Regulations, even if the contract would, apart from the choice of law, be governed by the law of another Member State. This outcome hardly seems consistent with the overall policy of minimum consumer protection which informs the Directive, particularly when it is recalled that the policy of section 27(1) was to avoid discouraging "foreign businessmen from agreeing to arbitrate their disputes in England or Scotland" (see Law Com. No.69 (1975), para.232), a policy which has little, if any, relevance to consumer protection. It would be most consistent with the policy of the Directive not to apply section 27(1) at all where the applicable law in the absence of choice is the law of a Member State. If it is not possible to do this, further problems will arise concerning the relationship between the subsection and Articles 3(3) and 5 of the Rome Convention (above, para.1–041) as discussed in *Benjamin*, para.25–093.

Title, commencement and extent

1–050   **1.**—(1) These Regulations may be cited as the Sale and Supply of Goods to Consumers Regulations 2002 and shall come into force on 31st March 2003.
    (2) These Regulations extend to Northern Ireland.

General Note

1–051   The Regulations came into force on March 31, 2003, and accordingly applies to contracts concluded on (see the Interpretation Act 1978, section 4(a)) or after that date, whereas Article 11 of the Directive requires Member States to comply with the Directive not later than January 1, 2002. The failure to transpose the Directive by the prescribed date gives rise to the possibility of a claim in tort for damages against the United Kingdom government at the suit of a claimant who has incurred loss as a result: see, generally, Joined Cases C6 & 9/90 *Francovich and Bonifaci* v *Italy* [1991] E.C.R. I–5357, ECJ Case C–178/94 *Dillenkofer* v *Germany* [1997] Q.B. 259; [1996] E.C.R. I–4845, ECJ. However, this would assume practical importance only if the rules of United Kingdom law already operative gave a lower level of protection in the circumstances of the individual case and in most respects they are unlikely to be adjudged to do so. Situations in which it could be argued that implementation is less than complete are indicated at paras 1–013, 1–190 and paras 1–035 *et seq.*

Interpretation

2. In these Regulations—   **1–052**
  "consumer" means any natural person who, in the contracts covered by these Regulations, is acting for purposes which are outside his trade, business or profession;
  "consumer guarantee" means any undertaking to a consumer by a person acting in the course of his business, given without extra charge, to reimburse the price paid or to replace, repair or handle consumer goods in any way if they do not meet the specifications set out in the guarantee statement or in the relevant advertising;
  "court" in relation to England and Wales and Northern Ireland means a county court or the High Court, and in relation to Scotland, the sheriff or the Court of Session;
  "enforcement authority" means the Director General of Fair Trading, every local weights and measures authority in Great Britain and the Department of Enterprise, Trade and Investment for Northern Ireland;
  "goods" has the same meaning as in section 61 of the Sale of Goods Act 1979;
  "guarantor" means a person who offers a consumer guarantee to a consumer; and
  "supply" includes supply by way of sale, lease, hire or hire-purchase.

GENERAL NOTE

Regulation 2 (and in particular, the definition of "consumer"),   **1–053** although at first sight applicable to the entire Regulations, is in fact mainly linked to Regulation 15 and its provisions concerning consumer guarantees. The other Regulations operate by way of amendment to legislation, notably in the context of this work the Sale of

Goods Act 1979, which contains its own interpretation section. For example, the expression "deals as consumer" is, as already noted, defined in section 61(5A), by reference to Part I (in particular section 12) of the Unfair Contract Terms Act 1977 and not by reference to Regulation 2 of the present Regulations. The definition of the word "consumer" is considered below and the quite distinct definition of one who "deals as consumer" is considered in the context of Regulation 14 (see below, paras 1–250 *et seq.*). As has been noted (see above, para.1–001), the latter definition is by far the more important in the context of the Regulations as a whole.

CONSUMER

1–054   The definition of "consumer" as set out in Regulation 2 is now becoming common form in enactments concerning consumers. For example, the same form of words is used in the Unfair Terms in Consumer Contracts Regulations 1999 (SI 1999/2083), reg.3(1), and a close equivalent is used in the Consumer Protection (Distant Selling) Regulations 2000, (SI 2000/2334), reg.3(1).

1–055   The definition has two elements. Firstly, a "consumer" must be a "natural" person, thus excluding legal persons and hence bodies corporate. This interpretation is confirmed by the decision of the European Court of Justice in *Cape Snc* v *Idealservice Srl, Idealservice MN RE Sas* v *OMAI Srl* (Joined cases C–541/99 and C–542/99) [2002] All E.R. (EC) 657) in the context of Directive 93/13 on unfair terms in consumer contracts. On the facts of the case the Directive did not cover the supply to certain Italian companies of automatic drink dispensers to be installed on the premises for the use of their staff. The companies were not "natural persons" for the purposes of the Directive. The word "individual" might be used as an appropriate synonym for "natural person" and indeed it is so used in Regulation 14, which amends section 12 of the Unfair Contract Terms Act 1977 (see below, para.1–250 *et seq.*).

1–056   The second element is that a natural person (for example, a sole trader or a partner) would not be within the definition unless he is "acting for purposes which are outside his trade, business or profession". The equivalent words in Article 1.2(a) of the Directive are "purposes which are not related to" his trade, business or profession. It is notoriously difficult to predict what is excluded by such limiting words. For example, if the acquisition of the vending machine in the *Cape Snc* case noted above had been by a sole trader he would probably *not* have acquired it in the course of a business for the purposes of section 12(1)(a) of the Unfair Contract Terms Act 1977 and so could (in the light of the amendments introduced by Regulation 14, below) be regarded as dealing as consumer for the purposes of that Act (see *Benjamin*, para.13–071 and cases there cited). Yet were he to re-sell the machine the sale would be treated as being in the course of a business for the purpose of attracting the implied conditions as to satisfactory quality, etc. of section 14 of the Sale of Goods Act 1979 (see *Stevenson* v *Rogers* [1999] Q.B. 1028 and *Benjamin*, para.11–045).

The words "outside" and "not related to" appear to indicate that if a   1–057
person is to be treated as a consumer in the context of Regulation 2 and Article 1.2(a) the transaction must have had no connection with his business. On that basis a person acquiring the vending machine in the above example would not do so as a "consumer" and the same would be true of cases where goods are acquired partly for business and partly for private use. In their memorandum to the House of Lords Select Committee to which reference was made above (at para.1–002) Professors Beale and Howells observed (see p.2 of the Minutes of Evidence) that the principal architect of the Directive, Mr Tenreiro, had envisaged that the use of the words "directly related to" in an earlier version of the definition would exclude only purchasers who intend to resell or let third parties use the goods with a view to profit. However, the omission of the word "directly" from the final version suggests a meaning which would exclude a much wider category. This would lead to a further divergence between the meaning of the term "consumer" (as used in Regulation 2 and thus Regulation 15: see below, paras 1–260 *et seq.*) and the notion of "dealing as consumer" (as used in Regulations 3 to 5 and elsewhere: see above, paras 1–024—1–026, below, paras 1–250 *et seq.*). Some divergence is inevitable as the one is limited to natural persons or individuals, whereas the other is not. From the standpoint of general policy, there are no obvious justifications for construing the category of persons who might benefit from the very modest provisions of Regulation 15 narrowly. On the other hand, there are clear and probably compelling reasons for construing a common form definition consistently so as to ensure that it has the same meaning in whatever enactment it is being used. An interpretation whereby a person would be acting as a "consumer" only if the relevant transaction is exclusively for a non-business purpose would be more in accord with the wording of the definitions.

CONSUMER GUARANTEE

The definition of "consumer guarantee" is modelled closely on the   1–058
definition of "guarantee" contained in Article 1.2(e) of the Directive. This makes it clear that the undertaking may be that of the producer

(manufacturer) of the goods or their retail seller. It is substantially certain that the words "acting in the course of his business" will be construed in the same sense as in section 14 of the 1979 Act and hence as including guarantees linked to sales which are essentially incidental to the main activities of the guarantor (see *Stevenson* v *Rogers* [1999] Q.B. 1028 and *Benjamin*, para.11–045). The reference to the undertaking being given "without extra charge" is apt to exclude extended warranties (for example, in relation to electrical equipment) for which an additional payment is required. In effect, these operate as a type of insurance cover. A relatively recent examination of the costs and benefits of such warranties is to be found in an Office of Fair Trading paper, *Extended Warranties on Domestic Electrical Goods* (OFT 387, July 2002).

ENFORCEMENT AUTHORITY

1–059   It should be noted that section 1(1) of the Enterprise Act 2002 establishes a body corporate to be known as the Office of Fair Trading. Section 2(1) of that Act transfers the functions of the Director General of Fair Trading to that body and the office of the Director General is abolished by section 2(2). These provisions were brought into force on April 1, 2003: see the Enterprise Act 2002 (Commencement No.2, Transitional and Transitory Provisions) Order 2003, (SI 2003/766), Article 2 and Schedule. For further references to enforcement provisions, see below, para.1–267.

GOODS

1–060   The definition in section 61(1) of the Sale of Goods Act 1979 is printed in Appendix A and is discussed in detail in *Benjamin*, paras 1–078 *et seq.*

SUPPLY

1–061   The definition of "supply" is essentially the same as that contained in section 137(2) of the Fair Trading Act 1973. It should be read in the light of Article 1.2(c) of the Directive which defines a "seller" as "any natural or legal person who, under a contract, sells consumer goods in the course of his trade business or profession."

Additional implied terms in consumer cases

1–062   **3.**—(1) Section 14 of the Sale of Goods Act 1979 is amended as follows.

(2) After subsection (2C) insert—

"(2D) If the buyer deals as consumer or, in Scotland, if a contract of sale is a consumer contract, the relevant circumstances mentioned in subsection (2A) above include any public statements on the specific characteristics of the goods made about them by the seller, the producer or his representative, particularly in advertising or on labelling.

(2E) A public statement is not by virtue of subsection (2D) above a relevant circumstance for the purposes of subsection (2A) above in the case of a contract of sale, if the seller shows that—

   (a) at the time the contract was made, he was not, and could not reasonably have been, aware of the statement,

   (b) before the contract was made, the statement had been withdrawn in public or, to the extent that it contained anything which was incorrect or misleading, it had been corrected in public, or

   (c) the decision to buy the goods could not have been influenced by the statement.

(2F) Subsections (2D) and (2E) above do not prevent any public statement from being a relevant circumstance for the purposes of subsection (2A) above (whether or not the buyer deals as consumer or, in Scotland, whether or not the contract of sale is a consumer contract) if the statement would have been such a circumstance apart from those subsections."

PUBLIC STATEMENTS REGARDING THE GOODS

1–063 Regulation 3 amends section 14 of the Sale of Goods Act 1979 in cases where the buyer "deals as consumer" (see above, paras 1–024 *et seq.* and below, paras 1–250 *et seq.*) by inserting three extra subsections after subsection (2C). They are as set out above:

1–064 Section 14 of the Sale of Goods Act deals with satisfactory quality, and contains (in subsection (2B)) five guidelines to take into account as aspects of the quality of goods (see *Benjamin*, paras 11–024 *et seq.*). The guidelines were added as part of the reforms of 1994 and making these matters specific was largely in the interests of consumers. A matter which was not then dealt with, however, and on which there was little precise authority, was the relevance of statements made about the goods, whether by the manufacturer in advertising or on the labelling of the goods or in booklets of instructions; or by a distributor in the same ways; or by the seller himself.

1–065 Such statements when made by the seller might be contractual promises, or misrepresentations inducing the contract. When made by a manufacturer or distributor they might be relevant to the description of the goods even when sold by others (*e.g.* a substance labelled as a "cough mixture" which would have no effect on coughs and hence would not be cough mixture at all). They might also indicate the description of the goods to which the quality provisions are then to be applied, for instance where goods are described as "cleaning fluid" but actually, though the fluid certainly cleans, it is unsafe because of excess acidity, so is not of satisfactory quality, or car polish is polish but does not provide the rust protection claimed. However, there was no clear guidance as to when such statements were to be taken into account in the application of the normal rules and criteria in this way, and this was especially so when claims were made in general advertising.

1–066   The above provision now directs that such matters are to be taken into account when the buyer deals as consumer. In accordance with the requirements of Article 2.2(d) of the Directive, which links them with quality and performance, they are only to be taken into account as regards whether the goods are of satisfactory quality. The relevance of such statements to pure matters of the description of the goods is not affected and remains covered by existing reasoning, and indeed section 14(2F) makes this clear. It is to be noted that such statements are not added as part of a new guideline, but as part of the "relevant circumstances" in the general definition, which requires that satisfactory quality be ascertained by taking account of any description of the goods, the price (if relevant) and "all the other relevant circumstances". This is doubtless because such statements cannot easily be regarded as "*aspects* of the quality of the goods" to which the guidelines are relevant.

1–067   The meaning of this provision is fairly self-explanatory, but argument may no doubt arise as to what is a "public statement" (though some guidance is given by the reference to advertising or labelling; the former no doubt includes television and radio advertising and posters); and "specific characteristics."

1–068   The statements must be made by "the seller, the producer or his representative". "Producer" is defined in Regulation 6, amending section 61(1) of the 1979 Act, as meaning "the manufacturer of goods, the importer of goods into the European Economic Area or any person purporting to be a producer by placing his name, trade mark or other distinctive sign on the goods." (see below, para.1–225).

The European Economic Area consists of the EU countries with the addition of Norway, Iceland and Liechtenstein. The words "or his representative" are puzzling: whose representative? The normal

grammatical construction would be that only the producer's representative is referred to. This seems to omit cases where the statements are
made by a representative of the seller; but perhaps these will be dealt
with under the general law of agency as statements of the seller himself. It is then not clear why the same reasoning could not be used of
the producer's representative, unless it be thought that agency reasoning is confined to contract situations. The word "representative" is
imprecise even if no other word would obviously be better, and it may
give rise to argument.

The criteria in subsection (2E) seem fairly obvious, and the idea of   **1–069**
public correction would refer primarily to a withdrawal in the same
medium, or the same level of publicity as that used for the statement in
the first place. Situations could certainly arise, however, where a withdrawal of a statement would require more publicity than the original
statement itself. It should be noted that it is the seller who has to show
these features, since it is his liability under section 14(2) that is in issue;
and that subsection (2C)(c) requires that the decision to buy *could not*
have been influenced by the statement. This prevents arguments
about whether it *was* so influenced, and makes the burden of proof on
the seller a strong one.

Subsection (2F) simply preserves the possibilities of such statements   **1–070**
being relevant to the seller's duties under the existing rules, as adum-
brated above, and indicates that the substance of section 14(2D) and
(2E) may, on appropriate facts, be applicable where the buyer does
not deal as consumer.

ARTICLE 2.3 OF THE DIRECTIVE

In this connection it may be noted that between the two provisions of   **1–071**
the Directive which require compliance with public statements,
Article 2.2(d) and 4, appears a provision to different effect. This is
Article 2.3, which reads:

> "There shall be deemed not to be a lack of conformity for the purposes of   **1–072**
> this Article if, at the time the contract was concluded, the consumer was
> aware, or could not reasonably be unaware of, the lack of conformity, or if
> the lack of conformity has its origin in materials supplied by the
> consumer."

Though such a proposition is fairly obvious it is not in fact clear that   **1–073**
the wording of section 14 of the Sale of Goods Act specifically
achieves this result. If a consumer claims under section 14(3) (*Benjamin*, paras 11–064 *et seq.*), regarding fitness for particular purpose, it
would seem fairly clear that the matters mentioned in Article 2.3

would make it unreasonable for the buyer to rely on the seller's skill or judgment: hence there would in such a case be no breach of section 14(3).

1–074   But section 14(2), imposing a general standard of satisfactory quality (*Benjamin*, paras 11–026 *et seq.*), does not in so many words deal with the matters referred to in Article 2.3, because the exceptions are phrased to cover only matters specifically drawn to the buyer's attention, and those which would in a sale by sample have been apparent on reasonable examination of the sample. It does not, therefore, in so many words, deal with situations where the defect in the goods was or should have been known to the buyer for other reasons. It seems possible however to say that such situations are covered by the general words of section 14(2A), requiring the goods to "meet the standard that a reasonable person would regard as satisfactory, taking account of any description of the goods, the price (if relevant) and all the other relevant circumstances." This would require the "reasonable person" to be one who has all information available to the actual buyer, and not merely a reasonable bystander. It is submitted in *Benjamin* (para.11–049) that this is the correct interpretation. Even if this is not so, any omission would be adverse to the seller, not the consumer, and so would not involve non-compliance with the Directive. Where the problem arises because the buyer supplies some of the materials, there is in any case less difficulty: see *Benjamin*, para.11–060.

Amendments to rules on passing of risk and acceptance of goods in consumer cases

1–075   4.—(1) Section 20 of the Sale of Goods Act 1979 is amended as follows. For the marginal note there is substituted "Passing of risk".

(2) After subsection (3) there is inserted—

"(4) In a case where the buyer deals as consumer or, in Scotland, where there is a consumer contract in which the buyer is a consumer, subsections (1) to (3) above must be ignored and the goods remain at the seller's risk until they are delivered to the consumer."

(3) In section 32 of the Sale of Goods Act 1979, after subsection (3) there is inserted—

"(4) In a case where the buyer deals as consumer or, in Scotland, where there is a consumer contract in which the buyer is a consumer, subsections (1) to (3) above must be ignored, but if in pursuance of a contract of sale the seller is authorised or required to send the goods to the buyer, delivery of the goods to the carrier is not delivery of the goods to the buyer."

GENERAL NOTE

This regulation alters the law relating to the risk of loss, destruction,   **1–076**
damage or deterioration of goods that are the subject-matter of a contract of sale in situations where the buyer "deals as consumer" (as
defined in section 61(5A) of the 1979 Act and discussed in the Introduction and General Note above). The general effect of the amendment is that, in such a case, risk will no longer pass with the transfer of
the property in the goods to the buyer or on delivery of the goods to a
carrier for transmission to the buyer, but only on delivery of the goods
to the buyer.

COMPLIANCE WITH THE DIRECTIVE

It is somewhat surprising that this amendment has been made to the   **1–077**
existing law by the Regulations. No proposal for such a change was
included in either the First or the Second Consultation Papers in January 2001 and February 2002. Article 2.1 of the Directive requires that
"the seller must deliver goods to the consumer that are in conformity
with the contract of sale" and Article 3.1 provides that the seller is to
be liable to the consumer for any lack of conformity "which exists at
the time the goods were delivered". The inference to be drawn from a
literal reading of these provisions is that the goods must be in conformity with the contract of sale at the time of delivery and not, for
example as under Article 36.1 of the Vienna Convention on the International Sale of Goods, when the risk passes to the buyer. It is therefore arguable that it was necessary to alter the law relating to risk in
order to comply fully with the Directive. However, the Directive contains no provisions on risk and para.(14) of the preamble to the Directive specifically states that the references to the time of delivery do not
imply that the Member States have to change their rules on the passing of the risk. In any event, the amendments to the existing law go
beyond any arguable requirements of the Directive. For instance,
where the buyer deals as consumer, the risk of loss or destruction of
the goods will remain with the seller until they are delivered to the
buyer whereas the most that the Directive would require is that the
risk of damage to or deterioration of the goods rendering them not in
conformity with the contract should remain with the seller until that
time. It is therefore submitted that it was not necessary to include
Regulation 4 in order to comply with the Directive. Nevertheless, it is
suggested that the regulation is not *ultra vires* as it is sufficiently
related to the subject-matter of the Directive to justify its inclusion as
permitted by section 2(2) of the European Communities Act 1972 and
Article 8.2 of the Directive.

[29]

AMENDMENT OF SECTION 20 OF THE 1979 ACT

1–078 Subsections (1) to (3) of section 20 of the 1979 Act provide as follows—

> "(1) Unless otherwise agreed, the goods remain at the seller's risk until the property in them is transferred to the buyer, but when the property in them is transferred to the buyer the goods are at the buyer's risk whether delivery has been made or not.
>
> (2) But where delivery has been delayed through the fault of either buyer or seller the goods are at the risk of the party at fault as regards any loss which might not have occurred but for such fault.
>
> (3) Nothing in this section affects the duties or liabilities of either seller or buyer as a bailee or custodier of the goods of the other party."

1–079 The new subsection (4) provides that, where the buyer deals as consumer, two consequences follow: first, "subsections (1) to (3) ... must be ignored", and, secondly, "the goods remain at the seller's risk until they are delivered to the consumer".

Effect of ignoring subsection (1) of section 20

1–080 The effect of ignoring subsection (1) of section 20 is that, where the buyer deals as consumer, there is no longer any presumption (see *Benjamin,* para.6–002) that risk passes with property. The well-established rule of the common law that the owner bears the risk (*res perit domino*) ceases to apply. So, for example, if a car dealer sells unconditionally to a private buyer a specific motor car which, at the time of the contract, is in a deliverable state, property in the car will pass to the buyer under section 18, rule 1 of the 1979 Act when the contract is made, and it is immaterial whether the time of delivery or the time of payment, or both, be postponed (see *Benjamin,* para.5–016). But the risk will no longer pass to the buyer at the same time. It will pass only on delivery of the car to the buyer. This may well accord better with the common assumption of both buyer and seller in a modern consumer transaction.

Conversely, where the seller allows the buyer to have possession of the goods agreed to be sold but reserves the right of disposal, for example, by retaining title to the goods until the price is paid (see *Benjamin,* para.5–131), the effect of ignoring subsection (1) is that it will no longer be presumed (unless otherwise agreed) that the risk remains with the seller merely because the property in the goods has not yet been transferred to the buyer. In such a case, although it could be argued that, by allowing the buyer to have possession of the goods before payment, the seller has "delivered" the goods and so passed the risk to the buyer, it is submitted that this is not the case. Possession of the goods will have been given to the buyer as bailee and there will be no "delivery" to the buyer in the technical sense of that word until the property passes to the buyer since it is only then that he will cease to hold the goods as bailee on behalf of the seller and commence to hold them on his own account (see *Benjamin,* para.8–011). The effect of ignoring subsection (1) will, therefore, not produce any substantially different result in this situation.

Where the contract is one for the sale of unascertained goods, property will be transferred from the seller to the buyer under section 18, rule 5 of the 1979 Act when the goods are unconditionally appropriated to the contract by one party with the assent of the other (see *Benjamin,* para.5–068); but the effect of section 20(4) is that, where the buyer deals as consumer, the risk will pass to him only on delivery. So, for example, where a private buyer orders a vacuum cleaner from a department store, the risk will not pass when the vacuum cleaner arrives and is placed in the stock room labelled with the buyer's name or even when he is notified that it is ready to be collected, but only when it is delivered to him. Also, under section 20A of the Act (see *Benjamin,* para.5–109), where there is a contract for the sale of a specified quantity of unascertained goods forming part of an identified bulk, a pre-paying buyer will have transferred to him property in an undivided share in the bulk and he will become an owner in common of the bulk. Again, however, where the buyer deals as consumer, the risk will pass to him only on delivery. So, where a private buyer agrees to buy one case of wine from a number of cases of the same wine lying in a particular cellar, and pre-pays the price, though he may acquire the property in an undivided share of all the wine of that description in the cellar and become an owner in common with others of that wine, nevertheless the risk will pass only when a case is separated from the bulk of the remaining cases and delivered to him.

Effect of ignoring subsection (2) of section 20

Under subsection (2) of section 20, if, for example, the goods sold are **1–081** perishable goods and the buyer delays taking delivery of them beyond the due date for delivery, the risk of any deterioration of the goods which would not have occurred but for the delay must be borne by the buyer (*Demby Hamilton & Co Ltd v Barden* [1949] 1 All E.R. 435; see *Benjamin,* para.6–019). It is difficult to see why it has been thought necessary to provide that this fair and salutary provision should be ignored where the buyer deals as consumer. The effect of ignoring subsection (2) in such a case means that the risk of deterioration remains with the seller even though the deterioration has been brought about by the buyer's delay. The seller will therefore be liable if, because of the delay, the goods have so deteriorated that they are not in conformity with the contract. This does not seem to be a reasonable result.

1–082   The seller may, however, not be without a remedy in this situation. If the contract of sale expressly or impliedly fixes a time at or within which the buyer must take delivery of the goods, and if that time is of the essence of the contract (see *Benjamin,* para.9–005), then any delay by the buyer in taking delivery may be treated by the seller as a repudiation of the contract and entitle him to claim damages from the buyer for non-acceptance under section 50 of the Act. Further, section 37(1) of the Act provides—

> "When the seller is ready and willing to deliver the goods, and requests the buyer to take delivery, and the buyer does not within a reasonable time after such request take delivery of the goods, he is liable to the seller for any loss occasioned by his neglect or refusal to take delivery, and also for a reasonable charge for the care and custody of the goods"

Although in practice this section is more usually relied on to recover storage charges expended or incurred by the seller (see *Benjamin,* para.9–009), the words "he is liable to the seller for any loss occasioned by his neglect or refusal to take delivery" could extend to loss to the seller resulting from deterioration of the goods due to a delay in taking delivery while the goods were at the seller's risk.

Effect of ignoring subsection (3) of section 20

1–083   Ignoring subsection (3) of section 20 would appear to have no discernible effect. Where one party, whether buyer or seller, is in possession as bailee of goods owned by the other, he will in any event be under an obligation as bailee to take reasonable care of the goods.

"Goods remain at the seller's risk until they are delivered to the consumer"

1–084   With respect to the second of the two consequences provided for in the new subsection (4), it would be possible to construe these words as meaning no more than that the risk remains with the seller until *at least* the goods have been delivered to the buyer, but not as intending to lay down any positive rule that risk is to pass to the buyer on delivery. However, such a construction would leave a hiatus in the 1979 Act as there would then not be even a *prima facie* rule as to the time at which risk passes where the buyer deals as consumer. The words should therefore be construed as establishing a positive rule: that the goods will no longer be at the seller's risk, and will be at the buyer's risk, when delivered to him.

The reference to "the consumer" in the new subsection (4) appears to be a misprint for "the buyer" since "consumer" is not defined in the 1979 Act and only appears in the expression "deals as consumer" (which is defined).

Effect of the risk remaining with the seller until delivery

The effect of the risk remaining with the seller until the goods are   **1–085** delivered to the buyer is that, where they are damaged or deteriorate before delivery so that, for example, they are not of satisfactory quality or not reasonably fit for their purpose at the time of delivery, the buyer will be entitled to reject the goods and treat the contract as repudiated for breach of condition or to invoke the new remedies for non-conformity conferred by Part 5A of the Act (see below). Where the goods are lost or destroyed before delivery, the seller will – unless he can obtain replacement goods within the time limited for delivery – normally be liable to the buyer for damages for non-delivery under section 51 of the 1979 Act. But this will not be the case where section 7 of the Act applies. Section 7 applies (see *Benjamin,* para.6–029) where the goods agreed to be sold are "specific goods" (as defined in section 61(1) of the Act: see *Benjamin,* para.1–113) which perish before delivery and before the property in them has passed to the buyer, provided that this is not due to any fault on the part of the buyer or seller. In this situation, the contract of sale is avoided and both parties are released from all obligations that have not yet accrued at the time at which the goods perish (see *Benjamin,* para.6–033). It would appear that, to "perish", the goods need not have been totally destroyed, provided that they have been so altered in nature by damage or deterioration that they have become for business purposes something other than that which is described in the contract of sale.

Refusal of the buyer to take delivery

Since the risk passes to the buyer only on delivery where the buyer   **1–086** deals as consumer, the question arises as to the effect of the amendments made by Regulation 4 on the incidence of risk in the case of a refusal by the buyer to take delivery. If the seller tenders delivery of the goods to the buyer, but the buyer wrongfully refuses to take delivery, it is arguable that the seller could treat the delivery as having been duly made and the risk would pass to the buyer from that time. Alternatively the seller could treat a refusal to take delivery as a repudiation of the contract of sale, terminate the contract and claim damages from the buyer for non-acceptance under section 50 of the

Act. Damages under section 37(1) of the Act (see above) might also be available.

Meaning of "delivered"

1–087   Delivery is defined in section 61(1) of the 1979 Act, unless the context otherwise requires, to mean:

> "voluntary transfer of possession to another except that in relation to sections 20A and 20B ... it includes such appropriation of goods to the contract as results in property in the goods being transferred to the buyer".

It is important to appreciate that delivery does not necessarily involve the transfer of the actual physical custody of the goods by the seller to the buyer. Delivery can be actual or constructive. There may be a delivery of goods to the buyer even though they never leave the physical possession of the seller. Where a seller in possession of the goods sold acknowledges that he is holding the goods on account of the buyer in circumstances where he recognises the buyer's right to possess as owner and his continuing to hold the goods thereafter as the bailee with possession derived from that right, then the transaction amounts to "delivery" to the buyer immediately followed by redelivery to the seller as bailee (*Michael Gerson (Leasing) Ltd v Wilkinson* [2001] Q.B. 514; see *Benjamin,* para.8–009). The risk will therefore pass to the buyer when the acknowledgment occurs. Thus in the example given above of a sale of a car by a car dealer to a private buyer, it may not be necessary for the car to be physically handed over to the buyer for the risk to pass. The risk can pass by virtue of an acknowledgment even though the car remains throughout in the physical possession of the seller.

Similarly, where the goods at the time of sale are in possession of a third person, delivery will be held to have taken place if the third person acknowledges to the buyer that he holds the goods on his behalf (section 29(4) of the 1979 Act; see *Benjamin,* para.8–012). It is not necessary for physical possession of the goods to be given to the buyer and risk will pass to the buyer at the time of the acknowledgment.

Transfer of physical possession of the goods is also unnecessary in cases of symbolic delivery (see *Benjamin*, para.8–008). The paradigm example of symbolic delivery is the handing to the buyer of the key to the warehouse or other place where the goods sold are stored. It may be that symbolic delivery is only effective in relation to sales of goods where the goods are, in the words of Lord Kenyon "ponderous and incapable of being handed over by one person to another" (*Chaplin v Rogers* (1801) 1 East 192, 195). If so, symbolic delivery is unlikely to apply in a consumer transaction. But it is possible that the handing over by the seller to the buyer of the ignition key of a motor vehicle or the key to a safe deposit box might be held to be symbolic delivery of the vehicle or of the contents of the box, and the risk would pass to the buyer at that time.

It should also be noted that it may be agreed that delivery shall be made by the seller, not to the buyer himself but to a third person nominated by the buyer, and delivery to the third person then constitutes delivery of the goods to the buyer (*Four Point Garage Ltd v Carter* [1985] 3 All E.R. 12; see *Benjamin,* para.8–007). Further, if the seller is required to deliver the goods at the premises of the buyer, he discharges his obligation if he delivers them there without negligence to a person apparently having authority to receive them (*Galbraith and Grant Ltd v Block* [1922] 2 K.B. 155; see *Benjamin,* para.8–023). There is no reason to suppose that the new section 20(4) makes any alteration to the law on these two points where the buyer deals as consumer.

The reference in the definition of delivery in section 61(1) to sections 20A and 20B of the 1979 Act has no relevance to the passing of risk. Section 20A deals with undivided shares in goods forming part of a bulk (see above) and section 20B with the deemed consent by a co-owner to dealings in bulk goods (see *Benjamin,* para.5–124). For the limited purpose of interpreting the word "delivery" in section 20A(5) and 20B(1) an appropriation which passes the property in the goods to the buyer is equated with physical delivery. This has no effect on risk.

AMENDMENT OF SECTION 32 OF THE 1979 ACT

Subsections (1) to (3) of section 32 of the 1979 Act provide as follows: **1–088**

"(1) Where, in pursuance of a contract of sale, the seller is authorised or required to send the goods to the buyer, delivery of the goods to a carrier (whether named by the buyer or not) for the purpose of transmission to the buyer is prima facie deemed to be a delivery of the goods to the buyer.

(2) Unless otherwise authorised by the buyer, the seller must make such contract with the carrier on behalf of the buyer as may be reasonable having regard to the nature of the goods and the other circumstances of the case, and if the seller omits to do so, and the goods are lost or damaged in the course of transit, the buyer may decline to treat the delivery to the carrier as delivery to himself or may hold the seller responsible in damages.

(3) Unless otherwise agreed, where goods are sent by the seller to the buyer by a route involving sea transit, under circumstances in which it

is usual to insure, the seller must give such notice to the buyer as may enable him to insure them during their sea transit; and if the seller fails to do so, the goods are at his risk during such sea transit."

1-089   The new subsection (4) provides that, where the buyer deals as consumer, two consequences follow: first, "subsections (1) to (3) ... must be ignored", and, secondly, "if in pursuance of a contract of sale the seller is authorised or required to send the goods to the buyer, delivery of the goods to a carrier is not delivery of the goods to the buyer".

Effect of ignoring subsection (1) of section 32 and of delivery to a carrier not being delivery to buyer

1-090   The effect of ignoring subsection (1) of section 32 is that, where the buyer deals as consumer, there is no longer any presumption that delivery to a carrier for the purpose of transmission to the buyer is to be treated as delivery to the buyer (see *Benjamin,* para.8–014). But the new section 20(4) does more than merely abolish the presumption. The abolition is supported by a declaratory rule that delivery of the goods to a carrier is *not* delivery of them to the buyer. As a result, the risk of loss of or damage to the goods during transit will remain with the seller since, under the new section 20(4), risk passes only on delivery of the goods to the buyer. It should, however, be noted that, if the buyer sends his own transport to collect the goods, that is not delivery to a "carrier" but delivery to the buyer himself, and the risk will be on the buyer during the transit.

A further consequence of this change in the law is that, where the buyer deals as consumer, the time when and the place where the buyer must be afforded a reasonable opportunity for examination of the goods under section 34 of the 1979 Act (see *Benjamin,* paras 12–041 and 12–043) is the time when and the place where they are delivered to the buyer and not (as in *Perkins v Bell* [1893] 1 Q.B. 193) where and when they are delivered to a carrier. Moreover, under subsections (2) and (5) of section 35 of the 1979 Act, since the buyer is not deemed to have accepted the goods under section 35(1) until he has had a reasonable opportunity of examining them, and since a material question in determining whether the buyer has accepted the goods after the lapse of a reasonable time under section 35(4) is whether he has likewise had a reasonable opportunity for examination, it follows that acceptance will normally be deferred until after the goods have been delivered to the buyer himself and not merely to a carrier. This is important because acceptance of the goods by the buyer ordinarily has the result that the breach of a condition to be fulfilled by the seller cannot be treated by the buyer as a ground for rejecting the goods and treating the contract as repudiated (see section 11(4)), although it does not affect the new remedies conferred by Part 5A of the Act (see below).

Effect of ignoring subsections (2) and (3) of section 32

This change in the law is merely consequential. Both subsections (2)   **1–091**
and (3) of section 32 in certain circumstances place the risk to the goods during transit in whole or in part on the seller even where it would otherwise be on the buyer (see *Benjamin,* paras 6–017, 8–015). But since, under the new subsection (4), where the buyer deals as consumer the risk while the goods are in transit remains with the seller, it is no longer necessary to have these provisions.

WHAT REGULATION 4 DOES NOT DO

Regulation 4 makes no change in the rules that govern the passing of   **1–092**
property (see *Benjamin,* Chapter 5). Property will pass to the buyer, whether or not he deals as consumer, as prescribed by sections 16 to 20A of the 1979 Act. In particular, property will continue to pass (provided the goods are then ascertained) on delivery to a carrier under section 18, rule 5(2), of the 1979 Act (see *Benjamin,* para.5–098) even though, where the buyer deals as consumer, delivery of goods to a carrier is not delivery of goods to the buyer.

 The Regulation does not require section 33 of the 1979 Act to be ignored, and it will continue to apply even where the buyer deals as consumer. That section provides—

 "Where the seller agrees to deliver them at his own risk at a place other than that where they are when sold, the buyer must nevertheless (unless otherwise agreed) take any risk of deterioration in the goods necessarily incident to the course of transit".

As a result of the new section 32(4), the general risk while the goods are in transit remains with the seller. Although the terms of section 33 only strictly apply to cases where the seller "agrees", either expressly or by implication, to assume the risk during transit, it is probable that the same rule applies where, under the normal rules as to passing of risk, the goods would be at his risk during transit (see *Benjamin,* para.6–018). So, for example, if it is agreed that bedding plants ordered by a private buyer are to be sent to him by post, he would be bound to accept them even if they have suffered such deterioration during transit that they are no longer of satisfactory quality provided that they have deteriorated only to the extent that bedding plants would necessarily deteriorate in the course of transit by post.

The Regulation does not alter the rule contained in section 43(1)(a) of the 1979 Act that the unpaid seller of goods loses his lien or right of retention in respect of them when he delivers the goods to a carrier for the purpose of transmission to the buyer without reserving the right of disposal of the goods (see *Benjamin,* para.16–046).

CAN THE PARTIES CONTRACT OUT OF THE ALLOCATION OF RISK EFFECTED BY THE AMENDMENTS?

1–093   Article 7.1 of the Directive provides that any contractual terms or agreements with the seller before the lack of conformity is brought to the seller's attention which directly or indirectly waive or restrict the rights resulting from the Directive shall, as provided by national law, not be binding on the consumer. It is submitted that this provision does not prevent the parties from agreeing, in appropriate cases, that the risk of loss or damage to the goods before delivery shall pass, in whole or in part, to the buyer and not remain with the seller as provided in the new section 20(4) and section 32(4) of the 1979 Act. In the first place, as argued above, the new provisions relating to postponement of the passing of risk until delivery of the goods to the buyer are not "rights resulting from this Directive". Secondly, in any event, English law as the national law would permit the parties by a contractual term or agreements to vary the incidence of risk in favour of the seller so as to exclude or restrict his liability for loss or damage to the goods provided that the term or agreement was reasonable (under sections 3 and 12 of the Unfair Contract Terms Act 1977) and was not unfair (under the Unfair Terms in Consumer Contracts Regulations 1999). It might be considered both reasonable and fair, even where the buyer deals as consumer, for the seller to stipulate that, should the buyer fail to take delivery of perishable goods on the due date, any deterioration of the goods thereafter should be at the risk of the buyer. And it might be regarded as both reasonable and fair, in a case where the goods are fragile and are required to be collected by the buyer from the seller's trade premises, for the seller to stipulate that should he be requested by the buyer to send them by carrier, then he will do so on condition that the buyer bears the risk of loss or damage during transit.

Buyer's additional remedies in consumer cases

5. After Part 5 of the Sale of Goods Act 1979 insert—   **1–094**

PART 5A

ADDITIONAL RIGHTS OF BUYER IN CONSUMER CASES

INTRODUCTION

A Part 5A with the above title is inserted into the Sale of Goods Act   **1–095**
1979 by Regulation 5. It seeks to implement the requirements of EU
Directive 1999/44/EC as to the consumer buyer's remedies for breach
of contract by the seller. The position at which this is inserted into the
Act is surprising. Part V of the Act concerns "Rights of Unpaid Sellers
against the Goods." Part VI deals with "Actions for Breach of the
Contract" and its first two subdivisions are headed "Seller's Remedies" and "Buyer's Remedies". It might be thought that it is after the
second subdivision that the changes now implemented by Part 5A
should appear, not after Part V, which concerns "Rights of Unpaid
Sellers against the Goods". This is the more so because the relevant
provision of the Directive, Article 3, is headed "Rights of the consumer." A minor point to note in this connection is that the number of
the new Part appears in Arabic figures, whereas the Sale of Goods Act
itself designates its Parts in Roman numerals, here Part V.

The requirements of the Directive are intended to standardise mini-   **1–096**
mal rights of the consumer buyer against his seller throughout the
European Union. (His rights against others such as the manufacturer
remain unchanged, as do the seller's remedies against his suppliers.)
The meaning of "consumer" is discussed elsewhere: (see above, paras
1–054 *et seq.*), but in the context of Part 5A it is the definition of the
expression "deals as consumer" which is the controlling factor which
may lead to the availability of the additional rights. This is discussed
above (see paras 1–024 *et seq.*) and, below (see paras 1–250 *et seq.*).

Article 2, entitled "Conformity with the contract", lays down the basic   **1–097**
duties of a seller to supply goods in conformity with the contract in
respect of description and quality, in a way very similar to the existing
requirements of English law as stated in sections 13 to 15 of the Sale of
Goods Act (which deal with conformity with description, quality and
conformity with sample). There are only two changes. The first relates
to public statements of the seller or certain others as to the character-

istics of the goods. Article 2.2(d) of the Directive requires that these shall be specifically mentioned as to be taken into account in assessing the "quality and performance which are normal in goods of the same type and which the consumer can reasonably expect". This has needed an implementing provision in the United Kingdom, adding such statements as relevant to the fulfilment of the Sale of Goods Act requirements as to satisfactory quality, contained in section 14(2). This is dealt with elsewhere: (see above, paras 1–063 *et seq.*). The second is the creation of a rebuttable presumption that goods which prove defective within six months of delivery were defective at the time of delivery. This is discussed below (paras 1–108 *et seq.*).

1–098   Article 3 of the Directive, "Rights of the consumer", is however a different matter. It appears to be intended to standardise the consumer's minimal remedies in a form familiar to civil lawyers. The form laid down is unfamiliar to, and hitherto never thought necessary by, the common law. This manifests itself in two principal ways. First, the civil law method of formulation of contractual remedies by considering first the duty to perform, in practice an order of the court that the contract or some part of it be performed, is followed. This remedy is therefore placed first in the list of remedies, and is the basis for giving the buyer what is for common law a new right to make an enforceable demand that the goods be repaired or replaced in certain circumstances.

1–099   Secondly, there follow modern versions of the romanistic remedies of reduction of the price (*actio quanti minoris*) and rescission (*actio redhibitoria*). The former remedy, which as an alternative to damages is relevant in rather special circumstances, is not known to the common law at all and no need has hitherto been found for it. The second is certainly part of the common law. But there the right referred to is, and has long there been, much more liberally granted as an application of general contract principles (under the titles "rejection" and "treating the contract as repudiated", and less often under that of "rescission") than is the present rescission remedy derived from romanistic systems of the law of sale. In the result that there has been no perceived need in common law countries for either of these special remedies in connection with sale.

1–100   This technique is partly that of the Vienna Convention on the International Sale of Goods (see *Benjamin*, para.1–024), and so will be familiar, even if (as is unlikely) it was not before, in many countries party to that Convention. The Convention, on which much has been written, is therefore of some value as a parallel, though comparisons must be made with caution as by Article 2(a) the Convention does not in general apply to sales of goods bought for personal, family or household use, and hence contains rules and emphases clearly directed towards commercial sales. In addition the Convention utilises throughout a more general notion of "fundamental breach of contract" instead of the more limited notion of rescission which is deployed in Part 5A.

But the United Kingdom is not a party to that Convention, which has **1–101** not arisen in litigation in the United Kingdom (and has not to any considerable extent in other common law countries adhering to it, such as the United States and Australia) in such a way as to attract attention. The incorporation of the new remedies required by the Directive into the general law of sale of goods, including the Sale of Goods Act 1979, and only in the context of consumer sales, must therefore have presented considerable problems for those drafting the Regulations. This is especially because there is (rightly) no intention to supersede the existing common law remedies of the buyer, which are in fact quite powerful, at any rate in theory. (The weakness lies in the difficulty of proving the existence of defects in the goods at the time of delivery, and perhaps in the cost of bringing legal proceedings).

It is indeed the intention of the Directive not to interfere with such **1–102** remedies. In Article 8 of the Directive it is provided that the rights resulting from it "shall be exercised without prejudice to other rights which the consumer may invoke under the national rules governing contractual or non-contractual liability;" and that "Member States may adopt or maintain in force more stringent provisions, compatible with the Treaty in the field covered by this Directive, to ensure a higher level of consumer protection." In accordance with this, Part 5A is entitled "*Additional* Rights of Buyer in Consumer Cases" (emphasis supplied); and no common law protection is anywhere reduced, let alone eliminated. Since the existing English law is often more stringent than the requirements of the Directive, few of the Directive's provisions were really needed in the United Kingdom.

Implementation of the Directive has required the insertion of parts **1–103** only of an alien regime which presupposes a different approach to that of common law. This has the potential to create considerable confusion. As its effect is to add further consumer remedies this is probably not as a matter of substance to the detriment of the consumer. But the cumulative effect of the two sets of rules will cause problems for anyone advising a consumer and may give somewhat surprising results on occasion. An important point for an adviser to bear in mind throughout is that the common law right to damages is in no way restricted and must apply in all the circumstances in which it would previously have applied, and possibly in a few more connected with the new remedies (*e.g.* where a buyer suffers loss while the goods are being repaired: below, para.1–125).

1–104 Some of the common lawyers involved in the drafting of the Vienna Convention were apt to say at the time that the special remedies of the civil law were rarely invoked, but that civil lawyers are familiar with and feel uneasy without them. Whether that is true or not, in a common law country they plainly require analysis as something separate alongside the existing remedies. The result is likely to prove complex, as will appear.

THE NEW PROVISIONS: SECTIONS 48A–48F

48A Introductory

1–105   (1) This section applies if—

      (a) the buyer deals as consumer or, in Scotland, there is a consumer contract in which the buyer is a consumer, and

      (b) the goods do not conform to the contract of sale at the time of delivery.

   (2) If this section applies, the buyer has the right—

      (a) under and in accordance with section 48B below, to require the seller to repair or replace the goods, or

      (b) under and in accordance with section 48C below—

         (i) to require the seller to reduce the purchase price of the goods to the buyer by an appropriate amount, or

         (ii) to rescind the contract with regard to the goods in question.

   (3) For the purposes of subsection (1)(b) above goods which do not conform to the contract of sale at any time within the period of six months starting with the date on which the goods were delivered to the buyer must be taken not to have so conformed at that date.

   (4) Subsection (3) above does not apply if—

      (a) it is established that the goods did so conform at that date;

      (b) its application is incompatible with the nature of the goods or the nature of the lack of conformity.

REMEDIES OF THE CONSUMER BUYER

1–106 This is an introductory provision which sets out by way of summary, rather in the same way as does Article 45 of the Vienna Convention, the consumer buyer's remedies, details of which are then given in subsequent sections.

When they apply

Subsection (1)(a) of section 48A limits the operation of the whole   **1–107**
section to situations where the buyer deals as consumer. The meaning
of this phrase is discussed elsewhere: (see above, paras 1–024 *et seq.*;
and below, paras 1–250 *et seq.*). Subsection 1(b) designates the section
as applying where the goods do not conform to the contract of sale at
the time of delivery. Such goods are often in ordinary speech referred
to as "defective" or "faulty" goods. The general notion of conformity
is set out in Article 2 of the Directive, but as stated above, most of its
provisions are regarded as identical to or less stringent than the existing requirements of English law and hence its requirements are in Part
5A defined in terms of compliance with the normal Sale of Goods Act
requirements as to description, quality and sample: see section 48F
below. As stated above, the quality stipulation has been amended so
as to require the taking into account of certain public statements made
concerning the goods. Reference to these is now incorporated into the
wording of section 14(2) of the Act: see above, paras 1–063 *et seq.* It
does not seem that the difference between "conformity *to* the contract" here and elsewhere, and "conformity *with* the contract" in the
heading to section 48F (below), is of significance.

Proof of and time factors relating to nonconformity

Section 48A(3), following Article 5.3 of the Directive, helps proof of   **1–108**
nonconformity by providing that goods which do not conform to the
contract of sale at any time within a period of six months starting with
the date of delivery "must be taken not to have so conformed at that
date." That the goods "must be taken not to have so conformed" is by
subsection (4) modified so as not to apply where it is established that
the goods *did* so conform at the relevant date; or if the application of
section 48A(3) is incompatible with the nature of the goods or the
nature of the lack of conformity. The first part of this proviso therefore creates, in effect, a presumption of nonconformity rebuttable by
the seller. The second deals with goods likely to deteriorate anyway,
in respect of which such a presumption would obviously be
inappropriate.

As compared with the common law regime this presumption may be   **1–109**
valuable. On normal reasoning, the right of the buyer to a remedy
depends on the goods having been defective at the time of delivery
(special variations on this where risk and property are separated are

by the Regulations made inapplicable to consumer contracts: see above, paras 1–076 *et seq.*). But it is often difficult for a claimant to establish the existence or inherence at the time of delivery of some defect which would have led to a subsequent deterioration. The seller may plausibly suggest that any deterioration which there is arises from natural wear and tear, misuse, lack of sufficient care, failure to maintain or service, or some other matter occurring after delivery, and this may be difficult to disprove. To do this it may, for example, be necessary to produce expert evidence that a particular item was of poor quality or design (taking its price into account); or of the likely durability of an Article of the type in question ("durability" being one of the guidelines laid down in section 14(2) of the Sale of Goods Act, the "satisfactory quality" provision: see *Benjamin*, para.11–052). The new presumption makes such arguments more difficult for the seller to employ because within the stated period it is he who must prove that the goods conformed on delivery: it is not for the buyer to disprove it.

1–110   The second part of subsection (4) has the effect that the presumption will not apply where the goods are such that they would not be expected to remain conforming for such a period (as in the case of flowers and many foodstuffs, and some cheap goods)—or that the lack of conformity was such that it would not have been present on delivery—as again in the case of foodstuffs, or a defect clearly caused by an event occurring after delivery. Such a limit on the presumption is obviously required.

1–111   There has been some tendency to represent this provision as creating a compulsory guarantee of quality for six months after delivery. This is not so: the question is simply one of proof of conformity on delivery, bearing in mind that disputes tend to arise later. The presumption assists the buyer in establishing that the goods did not conform at the relevant time, that of delivery. This is made clear by the exceptions to the presumption: plainly, many goods are perishable and could not be expected to remain of the same quality for six months. But in cases where the seller alleges fair wear and tear, misuse or maltreatment, the burden will now be on the seller to prove this rather than on the buyer to prove some lack of initial quality or durability.

1–112   Some of the official expositions of the Regulations point out that the seller may also prove accidental damage or loss after delivery. This is obviously true: proof of this would clearly be relevant to disproving an allegation by the buyer that the goods did not conform at the time of delivery. In such a situation, however, another problem can arise. It may be that this also prevents rejection by the buyer under the Act in general, on the basis that he cannot return the goods as they were. Whether it also prevents the buyer from rescinding under Part 5A is also not clear. Both these points are considered below: see paras 1–149, 1–150.

The rights conferred on the consumer buyer by Part 5A are then listed **1–113** as being those which require the seller to repair or replace the goods, to require the seller to reduce the purchase price, or to rescind the contract with regard to the goods in question. These are dealt with *seriatim* in sections 48B and 48C.

48B Repair or replacement of the goods

(1) If section 48A above applies, the buyer may require the seller—   **1–114**

    (a) to repair the goods, or

    (b) to replace the goods.

(2) If the buyer requires the seller to repair or replace the goods, the seller must—

    (a) repair or, as the case may be, replace the goods within a reasonable time but without causing significant inconvenience to the buyer;

    (b) bear any necessary costs incurred in doing so (including in particular the cost of any labour, materials or postage).

(3) The buyer must not require the seller to repair or, as the case may be, replace the goods if that remedy is—

    (a) impossible, or

    (b) disproportionate in comparison to the other of those remedies, or

    (c) disproportionate in comparison to an appropriate reduction in the purchase price under paragraph (a), or rescission under paragraph (b), of section 48C(1) below.

(4) One remedy is disproportionate in comparison to the other if the one imposes costs on the seller which, in comparison to those imposed on him by the other, are unreasonable, taking into account—

    (a) the value which the goods would have if they conformed to the contract of sale,

    (b) the significance of the lack of conformity, and

    (c) whether the other remedy could be effected without significant inconvenience to the buyer.

(5) Any question as to what is a reasonable time or significant inconvenience is to be determined by reference to—

(a) the nature of the goods, and
(b) the purpose for which the goods were acquired.

RIGHT TO REQUIRE REPAIR OR REPLACEMENT OF DEFECTIVE GOODS

1–115   This provision, like section 48C below, is of course an expansion of the introductory section 48A(2), that is to say, it applies in cases where the buyer deals as consumer and the goods do not conform to the contract of sale at the time of delivery.

Buyer's power to require repair or replacement

1–116   Section 48B confers on the buyer as a first remedy the power of requiring the seller to repair or replace the goods as appropriate, and provides that where such is required by the buyer the seller must repair or replace within a reasonable time, but without causing significant inconvenience to the buyer, and bear any necessary costs incurred in doing so, including in particular those of labour, materials or postage and no doubt other forms of carriage. Such repair or replacement may often occur in practice, but the existing common law does not confer a specific right to this effect. The power is therefore new. "Repair" is defined by Regulation 6, a new definition provision inserted into the definition section of the Sale of Goods Act, section 61(1), as "to bring the goods into conformity with the contract"; and the notion of conformity is dealt with in section 48F below.

The power is that of the buyer

1–117   Article 48 of the Vienna Convention gives the *seller* a power to remedy failure in performance even after delivery, and in some circumstances also to demand to know whether the buyer will accept such remedy. This is a notoriously controversial provision as its interaction with the buyer's right to "declare the contract avoided" is not clear. In the Directive and hence in these new Sale of Goods Act provisions, however, there is no indication of a right in the seller to demand to repair or replace the goods: the decision is that of the *buyer*. Section 48B simply says that the *buyer* "may" require the seller to do either of these things. However, if he does not do so, and the case is one where the new provisions would permit him to do so, it seems that the Part 5A remedies of reduction of the price or rescission will not be open to him: see section 48C(2) below. This may well sometimes yield a similar result to that where the seller has a right actually to demand to do these things. The seller can point out to the buyer that other remedies will not be available unless he first demands repair or replacement, and unless the seller is given an opportunity to effect this.

But if the remedy of rejection at common law is on general grounds **1–118** applicable, the buyer can reject on that basis without any such prelude—though if he has first sought repair or replacement (whether under this section or as a matter of practice) it is now provided that he cannot exercise the right until he has given a reasonable time for this to be done: see section 48D(1) below.

Exercise of the power

The exercise of the power is hedged around with restrictions which **1–119** will make its exercise, and hence the exercise of other remedies depending on its non-availability, not easy to establish if the matter is disputed. It is stated (see section 48B(3)) that the buyer "must" (rather than "may" in the previous subsection) not require repair or replacement in certain circumstances. The first doubt is as to the word "must". On normal principles of statutory construction this would seem to create a duty not to exercise a power which the buyer may normally exercise. The breach of such a duty would then be remediable in damages, though the power would be validly exercised. No doubt this was not intended, and one can only assume that the intention is that attempts to exercise the power are invalid in the circumstances indicated.

The circumstances in which the power "must" not be exercised are **1–120** then stated as occurring where the remedy is, first, impossible (subsection (3)(a)) or, second and third, disproportionate in particular respects (subsections (3)(b) and (c)). These criteria apply first to the choice between repair and replacement. One or the other of these may be impossible under (3)(a); or the exercise of one may be disproportionate to that of the other under (3)(b): for example, that of repair disproportionate to that of replacement, or that of replacement disproportionate to that of repair. The latter sort of case is obvious: often a repair might cost little, whereas a replacement could involve significant expenditure. But equally there may be cases of cheap electronic devices where replacement is easy but repair would be extremely expensive if not impossible.

Second, it is provided by subsections (3)(a) and (c) that the power may **1–121** not be exercised where the remedy would be impossible or disproportionate to the other remedies of reduction of price or rescission laid down in the following section, section 48C. If the exercise of the remedy is impossible, it is again excluded. As to disproportion, the remedies of reduction of price and rescission are themselves expressed to depend on the non-availability of the remedies of repair or replacement (or failure to carry them out), with the result that there is an element of circularity in the mechanism.

1–122   In many ways all this is a statement of common sense procedures followed by many buyers and sellers. But the balancing of these remedies, repair or replacement on the one hand, and reduction of the price or rescission on the other, is likely to lead to unpredictable results where there is a dispute as to what ought to or legitimately could have been done, especially where a dispute leads to the intervention of a court.

"Disproportionate"

1–123   Subsection (4) makes clear that whether the remedy is to be regarded as "disproportionate" is governed by its cost to the seller in comparison to whichever other Part 5A remedy is relevant, as well as the significance of the lack of conformity and the inconvenience likely to be caused to the buyer. That comparative cost is relevant is indeed assumed in the examples given above. There is no suggestion of a cost-benefit analysis between the cost to the seller and the *benefit* to the buyer. It is conceivable that this might be relevant to the question of "significant inconvenience" under section 48B(2)(a). See below, paras 1–124 *et seq*.

Reasonable time and significant inconvenience

1–124   Subsection (5) states in effect (and fairly obviously) that the phrases "reasonable time" and "significant inconvenience" are to be determined by the circumstances—the nature of the goods and the purpose for which they were acquired.

Cooperation by buyer

1–125   It is submitted that it is implicit in section 48B(2) that if the buyer does require the seller to repair or replace non-conforming goods he is under an obligation to facilitate the fulfilment of the seller's required action, *e.g.* to forward them to the seller where this is appropriate, allow the seller to have reasonable access to the goods, if the repair is to be made on the buyer's premises, or to allow the seller to take possession of the goods if they are to be repaired elsewhere, or if they are to be replaced. There is no express provision in Part 5A for the buyer to be compensated for his loss of the use of the goods during the period while they are being repaired or replaced, but since the common law right to damages is unaffected it seems that a common law claim for damages for this and other consequential loss would be available in addition to the repair or replacement remedy: see below, para.1–130. They would not be available for mere annoyance, disappointment or even distress (see *ibid*). If an order for specific performance is made by the court under section 48E(2) the court may possibly be able to impose a "condition" as to "damages" under section 48E(6): see para.1–184 below.

Repair—meaning

The duty to repair must be one of bringing the goods into conformity with the contract requirements. A simple example occurs where the buyer requires the seller to put right a defective speedometer in a car. The remedy is obviously more suitable to large and/or complex arte-facts such as cars and other machinery, and also for installed items which would be impracticable to return, such as a boiler. It is submit-ted that the fact that the repair may be expensive to the seller does not *necessarily* make a demand for repair disproportionate within section 48B(4). In the consumer context, the buyer should within reason be entitled to goods which satisfy him, and it would seem that there must be cases where such an entitlement does not have to yield to the argu-ment that a replacement will be more cost-effective to the seller.

1–126

Replacement—meaning

An obvious case for replacement is a cheap item of electronic goods which does not work and cannot easily be repaired. The buyer may demand its replacement. But there may be more difficult situations. If the goods are specific, for example a picture, and cannot be repaired, or repair is simply inappropriate, they clearly cannot be replaced with something else, albeit of a similar nature, which the buyer has not agreed to receive. Equally, if the reason why the goods do not con-form with the contract is because they are not suitable for their pur-pose under section 14(3) of the Sale of Goods Act, and it can be established that *no* goods of the type purchased or ordered would be so, replacement with the same sort of goods would clearly be an inap-propriate remedy. Difficulties may arise where the goods are second-hand or used when replacement is sought, or otherwise inferior to the norm. It would appear that replacement may, if this can be done, sometimes be effected by supplying a similar Article. Official docu-mentation in connection with the Regulations suggests that a five-year old piano with an inherent fault can be replaced with another of the same or similar specification. Since pianos and musical instru-ments, like second-hand cars, are usually tested and selected by the buyer and sold as specific goods, this particular example seems doubtful.

1–127

Enforcement

The obligation to repair or replace is secured by conferring on the court the power to make an order for specific performance of it. This is

1–128

effected by section 48E, discussed below (see paras 1–179 *et seq.*): it is doubtful whether any such power existed before. It should be noted that the court is not bound to make such an order, but under section 48E has the power to award another remedy under the Act if it thinks it appropriate.

Risk during repair or replacement

1–129   Where the goods are replaced they must presumably be at the seller's risk until the second delivery, that of the replacement goods: otherwise he cannot effect a replacement. But the question of risk while goods are in transit for repair, being repaired or in transit back from the repair operation is not mentioned. The general tenor of Part 5A, with its intention to protect consumers, suggests that all these are for the seller's account because they are caused by the initial nonconformity. If this is correct it would seem that if the goods for repair are entrusted to a normal method of carriage to the seller or someone designated by him, during which they are damaged or lost, the seller must still either repair them or replace them: and the same applies if loss or damage occurs while the seller is repairing them or sending replacement or repaired goods back to the buyer by a similar method of carriage.

Damages for loss of use during repair or replacement

1–130   When the seller fails to deliver a profit-earning chattel on the date fixed for delivery, but the buyer accepts delivery at a later date, the buyer may recover damages for loss of profits during the delay: (*Benjamin*, paras 17–039—17–042). By analogy, the consumer may in theory have a claim for damages if he can prove "loss" arising from his not having the use of the item while it is being repaired or replaced. But the consumer faces difficulties in proving any such "loss". If he actually incurs extra expense, such as hiring a car, during the period of non-use, he will be entitled to damages (subject to the usual rules of causation, remoteness and mitigation) on the ground of the breach of contract leading to the non-conformity: *Benjamin*, para.17–045. But if his only loss is annoyance, disappointment or frustration, the courts are most unlikely to award damages: *Benjamin*, paras 14–006, 16–046. Similarly, any short-lived "loss of amenity" suffered by the consumer is unlikely to entitle him to damages: (*Cf. Benjamin*, para.17–070).

48C Reduction of purchase price or rescission of contract

1–131   (1) If section 48A above applies, the buyer may—

      (a) require the seller to reduce the purchase price of the goods in question to the buyer by an appropriate amount, or

    (b) rescind the contract with regard to those goods,

if the condition in subsection (2) below is satisfied.

(2) The condition is that—

    (a) by virtue of section 48B(3) above the buyer may require nei-
ther repair nor replacement of the goods; or

    (b) the buyer has required the seller to repair or replace the goods,
but the seller is in breach of the requirement of section
48B(2)(a) above to do so within a reasonable time and without
significant inconvenience to the buyer.

(3) For the purposes of this Part, if the buyer rescinds the contract, any
reimbursement to the buyer may be reduced to take account of the
use he has had of the goods since they were delivered to him.

REDUCTION OF PURCHASE PRICE OR RESCISSION OF CONTRACT

These are two remedies which are new to the common law, though   **1–132**
rejection of the goods and termination of the contract for breach,
which in many respects is the same as what is here called "rescission"
and indeed referred to under this title in some textbooks, is of course a
well known common law procedure.

When remedies can be exercised

Subsection (2) makes clear that these remedies can be exercised only   **1–133**
in cases where the buyer does not have the power to require repair or
replacement, or the buyer has required repair or replacement but the
seller has not effected it within a reasonable time and without significant inconvenience to the buyer (section 48B(2)(3) above). The latter
notion of inconvenience to the buyer appears to envisage not only
situations where the seller cannot repair or replace without causing
such inconvenience, but also situations where he does repair or
replace, but significant inconvenience is nevertheless caused. Presumably what is meant is that the repair or replacement, even if tendered,
can be rejected by the buyer on the ground of such inconvenience. It
should be noted from the wording of section 48C(2)(b) that there is
apparently no need for the buyer to have recourse to a court order
before invoking the present remedies.

NATURE OF THE REMEDIES

(1) REDUCTION OF PURCHASE PRICE

Subsection (1)(a) provides that the buyer may require the seller to   **1–134**
reduce the purchase price of the goods in question to the buyer by "an

appropriate amount". (The French version states that the buyer "peut exiger une réduction adequate du prix"). On general principles it can be exercised even after the price has been paid. These words of subsection 1(a) are almost identical to the reference to this remedy in section 48A(2)(b)(i) above, save that that formulation omits the words "in question". The reason for this difference is not clear, but seems unlikely to be of significance.

1–135 The remedy of price reduction is new in English law but is widely available in European legal systems (see Lando and Beale eds., *Principles of European Contract Law* (2000), pp.430 *et seq.*) and as stated above derives from the Roman *actio quanti minoris*. The remedy assumes that the buyer accepts the seller's tender of performance even though the goods do not conform to the contract, so that performance is only partial. "The principle underlying price reduction is that the buyer may keep non-conforming goods delivered by the seller, in which case the contract is adjusted to the new situation: the price is reduced, just as if the subject-matter of the contract had from the outset been the non-conforming, less valuable goods actually delivered. Price reduction should therefore be regarded as an adaptation of the contract, not an award of damages": Schlechtriem, *Commentary on the UN Convention on the International Sale of Goods* (2nd ed., 1998), pp.437–438. Some simple examples in connection with the Vienna Convention are given by Nicholas in (1989) 105 L.Q.R. at pp.225–226

1–136 The lack of conformity may relate to quantity, quality, time of delivery (where this is an express term of the contract) or otherwise: see section 48F below. However, it is submitted that the remedy of price reduction will not be "appropriate" under section 48E(3) (below) if the goods are unable to perform the main function or purpose for which the buyer acquired them. In the case of defective quality, a price reduction is likely to be appropriate when the defect in the quality of the goods relates to an aspect of the goods which does not impede their use as intended by the buyer. For more serious defects in quality, the remedy of replacement or of termination (rescission) will be more appropriate.

(i) Analogies from the previous law

1–137 Before Part 5A was enacted, the Sale of Goods Act contained several provisions similar in effect to section 48C. An alternative to claiming damages for breach of warranty is the entitlement of the buyer to set up (by way of defence) the breach "in diminution or extinction of the price" (section 53(1): *Benjamin*, paras 17–046 and 17–048). The measure of damages for breach of warranty of quality is *prima facie* the difference between (a) the value of the defective goods at the time and place of delivery and (b) the value the goods would have had if they had fulfilled the warranty: (section 53(3): *Benjamin*, para.17–046). The concept of a "price allowance" has been used by the courts in applying this subsection (see *Benjamin*, para.17–052).

The new remedy may be an alternative to a claim for damages, but it might also lie where the seller is excused from liability in damages. (Special rules may however apply to frustration: *Benjamin*, paras 6–028 *et seq.*). If the price has not been paid, the new remedy of price reduction will operate as a set-off analogous to section 53(1) above. It is implicit in section 48C that the buyer who has already paid the price (or part of it) may recover from the seller any excess of the amount paid which exceeds the reduced price due after it has been reduced by the "appropriate" amount (*Cf.* Lando and Beale, *op.cit.* above, para.1–135, Article 9:401:2).   **1–138**

(ii) The amount of the reduction

By section 48C(1)(a), the amount of the price reduction is to be "appropriate". No guidance is given in Part 5A about the interpretation of this word. But the rules for the assessment of damages can provide an analogy for assessing the reduction. By section 53(3), the *prima facie* measure of damages for breach of a warranty of quality is the difference between the (lower) value of the defective goods at the time and place of delivery and the (higher) value the goods would then have had if they had fulfilled the warranty (or conformed to the contract). The price is fixed as at the time of contracting but this measure is assessed as at the time of delivery, by when the market price may have changed. But the comparison between the two values at the time of delivery could be used to fix the proportion of the price reduction, as is provided by Article 50 of the Vienna Convention ". . . the buyer may reduce the price in the same proportion as the value that the goods actually delivered had at the time of the delivery bears to the value that conforming goods would have had at that time." This provision finds the proportion by using the relative values at the time of delivery, but then applies that proportion to the original price.   **1–139**

The price is the ceiling from which the reduction is to be made, which means that the amount of the reduction could be less than the amount awarded as damages for breach (bearing in mind that damages can be awarded for consequential loss, which probably could not be used to assess an "appropriate price reduction"). Section 53(3) does not refer to the price, but to "the value the goods would have had if they had fulfilled the warranty". If the value of the goods has risen between the date of the contract and the date of delivery to the buyer, damages under section 53(3) will give the buyer a higher amount of compensation than price reduction, which takes "the price" as the ceiling. But if the value of the goods has fallen since the date of the contract, the price reduction remedy may produce a better remedy than damages. Section 53(3) puts on the buyer the risk of a decline in value after the contract, but on the seller the risk of a post-contract rise in value.

1–140   In some cases, the amount of the reduction could be easily calculated, *e.g.* if the quantity of items delivered to the buyer was short the reduction could be directly related to the proportion of the shortage in relation to the contractual quantity (*Cf.* section 30(1); *Benjamin*, para.8–045).

1–141   It must be remembered that damages continue to be available in respect of breach of contract. In view of this, it seems unlikely that the remedy of price reduction will be of much value unless either, as above stated, the ruling price for the goods bought has dropped between sale and delivery, which is obviously more likely to occur in a commercial context; or if the buyer has difficulty in proving damages, for example where he has bought the goods for a gift. It is however true that, at least in theory, the remedy does not require the intervention of a court.

(II) RESCISSION OF CONTRACT

Meaning

1–142   The word "to rescind" in section 48C(1)(b) is not explained. In the French version of the Directive the word is "résolution". In common law "rescind" is most usually taken as undoing the contract *ab initio*, usually in equity: see *Johnson v Agnew* [1980] A.C. 367. Hence there are "bars on the right to rescission": for example, it can be too late to rescind. It seems unlikely that this sense can be intended here, though the French word "résolution" (as opposed to "résiliation") suggests that it is. It is normally assumed that the word "rescinded" in s.48 of the Sale of Goods Act means no more than "terminated for breach" (see *Benjamin*, para.15–101). What seems to be meant in our present context is rejection of the goods, termination of the contract for breach and recovery of the price if paid.

1–143   Under section 36 of the Act a rejecting buyer has no need actually to return the goods: "it is sufficient if he intimates to the seller that he refuses to accept them." This must apply under Part 5A also. However, such an intimation or return of the goods will be important to preserve the buyer's rights, particularly if he may wish to rely on the six-month presumption (see above, para.1–108). Since the common law rights are not affected by Part 5A, actions for damages, which survive termination at common law, must survive here also.

However, termination (treating the contract as discharged for breach)   **1–144**
in a single performance contract, which is what most consumer contracts are, will usually have in any case a rescissory effect, in so far as in such a transaction the buyer must return the goods delivered and will normally be entitled to the return of the price in restitution as upon a total failure of consideration. But where the consumer is buying goods delivered by instalments the difference may be significant: it may be that instalments accepted can no longer be returned, and this makes the notion of "termination" more appropriate than that of "rescission".

Where the buyer seeks to recover the price paid for goods rejected,   **1–145**
whether in a single performance contract or an instalment contract, it may be argued that the whole price, or instalment price, could be recovered on the basis that the buyer has had nothing of what he contracted for, even if he has in fact had some or considerable use of the goods. This argument has been accepted at common law in relation to breach of the condition as to title contained in section 12(1) of the Sale of Goods Act: *Rowland v Divall* [1923] 2 K.B. 500 (see *Benjamin*, paras 4–006 *et seq.*). It is more doubtful in respect of defective quality, but the problem seems not to have arisen in this context, probably because of the comparatively short limits on the right to rescind put by the notion of acceptance.

But whether or not such reasoning could have been deployed at com-   **1–146**
mon law in the present situation, subsection (3) provides specifically that the reimbursement to the buyer may be reduced to take account of the use he has had of the goods since they were delivered to him. Short of a court order (which is envisaged by section 48E(5)) which is in virtually identical terms), the amount to be deducted can obviously be contentious between the parties; and the whole idea was rejected by the Law Commission in 1987 (see Law Com. No.160, Scot. Law Com. No.104, para.5.7) as taking away much of the force of the consumer buyer's bargaining position. However, such deduction is only to be made if the Part 5A rescission remedy is exercised. This rule only applies "for the purposes of this Part" and does not alter the position of a buyer who rejects the goods acting under his common law rights.

[55]

(i) Directive provision omitted

1–147   Article 3.6 of the Directive provides that "the consumer is not entitled to have the contract rescinded if the lack of conformity is minor." Such a restriction (in so far as it goes beyond the very limited operation of the *de minimis* principle) is alien to the common law: the word "minor" is to a common lawyer imprecise and the policy of the common law is to allow rejection for minor breaches of a contract term, express or implied. Any flexibility there may be comes in the initial application of the definition, where if a defect is sufficiently minor the goods may sometimes be held to conform with their description or be of satisfactory quality: a well-known commercial example is *The Hansa Nord* [1976] Q.B. 44 (*Benjamin*, para.11–041) though such reasoning would less easily be found in consumer cases. The reforms of 1994 introduced in a new section 15A a more precisely formulated exception to the right to reject, preventing its use where "the breach is so slight that it would be unreasonable for [the buyer] to reject them" (see *Benjamin*, paras 12–024 *et seq.*). This, however, is restricted to commercial sales and does not affect consumer sales, where it was regarded as important to preserve a strong right of rejection for consumers.

1–148   Article 3.6 is therefore inconsistent with United Kingdom policy in that it would actually reduce the consumer's protection and it may be presumed that this is why it was not implemented.

(ii) Rejection of damaged goods

1–149   The notion of rescission implies the return of the goods against a refund of the price (in English law at least), plus an award of damages where appropriate. What is nowhere made clear is whether rescission is possible when the goods cannot be returned at all, or cannot be restored in the condition in which they were on delivery. If this is due to a defect in the goods, that is of course something of which the seller cannot complain. This will also be true if part of the goods has been used up by normal testing (for example, tasting of wine) or normal installation (as where a roll of carpet is fitted). On the other hand, if it is due to misuse or mistreatment by the buyer, that he has lost the right to reject is obviously something of which he cannot complain.

1–150   There is, however, a third possibility. If the loss or damage was caused by something for which the buyer was not responsible, for example, purely accidental damage, can the buyer use this as an excuse for non-return, or return the damaged goods? Nothing in Part 5A gives guidance. The general English law is not clear either: (see *Benjamin*, paras 12–057—12–059). It is there suggested that the most likely view is that there can be no rejection (though an action for damages would lie); and if that is correct in general it should probably also apply here. The Vienna Convention makes specific provision for this problem in Article 82; but the wording of this is not easy to apply and hence not satisfactory as a guide, and even less so in consumer cases.

Instalment sales

The Sale of Goods Act approach to instalment sales is, where the con-   **1–151**
tract is severable, to regard each consignment as a separate delivery to which the normal rules for rejection apply. When the question arises as to whether delivery of defective instalments entitles the buyer to treat the whole contract as repudiated, this is governed by section 31(2) of the Act, which embodies a principle of the general law (see *Benjamin,* paras 8–063 *et seq.*). The new provisions do not address the problem, but there is nothing in them which suggests anything other than the same result as regards particular instalments; and it seems appropriate to treat the overall right to treat the whole contract as repudiated as governed by an application by analogy of the statement of the general law in section 31(2). The Vienna Convention here, as elsewhere, has the principle of "fundamental breach" on which to fall back: see Articles 51, 73.

Partial rejection

The reforms of 1994 introduced into the Sale of Goods Act by section   **1–152**
35A a right of partial rejection. The previous law had been that acceptance of any part of the goods barred rejection of the whole (subject to the instalment rules mentioned above). Now, where some of the goods conform, the buyer may if he wishes reject the whole consignment if the non-conformity is a breach of contract, but he may instead reject the defective parts of it (provided that what he rejects are "commercial units"; and provided that he accepts all the conforming goods) and keep the rest. So, a consumer buying a box ("case") of a dozen bottles of wine, and buying by the case rather than the bottle, who is able to ascertain without opening any that the contents of three bottles (or the bottles themselves) are defective may reject the case, or may reject the three bottles and retain the rest. Although this is not stated in the Act, he must presumably pay *pro rata* for the bottles he keeps; or if he has paid, he can recover back part of the price on a *pro rata* basis: (see *Benjamin*, para.12–061). There are complications regarding commercial contracts which are not likely to apply in consumer situations.

It is difficult to ascertain what the position is in such a situation under   **1–153**
the new remedies of sections 48A–48E. If "the goods" refers, as it

does in section 35A, to the goods tendered under the contract of sale, the buyer can presumably require replacement of the defective bottles. If this cannot be done (for example, because of the scarcity of the type of wine) or is not done, it would appear that the buyer can require the seller to reduce the purchase price of the goods in accordance with section 48C(1): in this context "the goods" presumably means the case delivered. Alternatively however he can "rescind the contract *with regard to those goods.*" The last five words or their equivalent are not used elsewhere in the Regulations, and it is not clear whether they simply allow partial rejection. The Directive, in the summary of remedies given by Article 3.2, also uses the words "rescinded with regard to those goods", which suggests partial rescission and hence rejection; but Articles 3.5 and 3.6 simply refer to having the contract rescinded (in the French version "la résolution du contrat") which might be taken to suggest that the whole consignment must be returned.

1–154 Under the Vienna Convention it is clear that the remedies only apply in respect of the defective part, but this is reinforced in Article 51.2 by a right to terminate the contract (declare it "avoided") where there is a fundamental breach, a general reasoning technique not found in the new sections of the Sale of Goods Act. The result under the Convention is said to be that the buyer may claim replacement of the defective goods, or rescind the contract in respect of them and reduce the overall purchase price; or keep the entire delivery and claim a price reduction, subject always to the doctrine of fundamental breach; (see Schlechtriem, *op.cit.* above, para.1–135, p.448). This would be a convenient result here also.

Quantitative shortages

1–155 Similar problems arise in connection with quantitative shortages. The Sale of Goods Act spells out the consequences of these specifically in section 30; and the right to terminate the contract overall is left to the general law on repudiatory breach. Under the new section 48F (see below) goods "do not conform to a contract of sale if there is, in relation to the goods, a breach of an express term of the contract or a term implied by sections 13, 14 or 15 above." The existence of the special rules in section 30 has meant that quantitative defects are not considered under section 13. However, a stipulation as to quantity, even if not to be regarded as going to description, would probably in any case be an express term of the contract for the purposes of section 48F: section 13 is indeed often criticised as stating what is actually an express term as an implied term. Similar considerations as those above seem likely to apply: the buyer may call for the making up of the quantity, assuming that this can be brought within the word "replacement": but if this procedure comes to nothing for the reasons given above, and reduction of the price is not sought or is inappropriate, the question whether the quantity supplied can be kept, or must be returned if the buyer rescinds, does not have a clear answer.

The position under the Vienna Convention is similar to that in respect **1–156** of delivery of partly defective goods. The buyer may demand the missing goods; or may rescind the contract in respect of that part, with consequent reduction of price: (see Schlechtriem, *op.cit.* above, para.1–135, pp.446–447). Again, there is the operation of "fundamental breach" in the background. There is a difference under that Convention, however, as the buyer is not entitled to reject part deliveries (Article 51.2) whereas under the Sale of Goods Act a buyer is (unless it is otherwise agreed) not under any obligation to receive delivery in instalments: section 31(1).

In the above two cases of partial rejection and quantitative shortages **1–157** (and elsewhere) it may well be that the buyer in the United Kingdom would do better to rely on the existing and known general law: see below.

RESTRICTIONS ON THE BUYER'S CHOICE OF A PART 5A REMEDY

The wording of sections 48B(1) and 48C(1) ("... the buyer may ...") **1–158** appears to give the buyer complete freedom to choose which remedy to "require" or exercise. But there are some explicit restrictions on his choice. For example, by section 48B(3), discussed above, repair or replacement must not be chosen if it is "impossible" or "disproportionate in comparison to" another of the four remedies. ("Disproportionate" is defined by section 48B(4) and (5): see above, para.1–123.)

The court has however an overriding power under section 48E **1–159** (below) to decide that "another remedy" than the one chosen by the buyer is "appropriate". This means that the buyer's initial choice of remedy must be made in the light of this power, which may substitute that other remedy for the one chosen by the buyer. The concept of one remedy being "disproportionate" under section 48B(4) and (5) is obviously one aspect of the decision whether a remedy is "appropriate", but the absence of any definition of "appropriate" gives the court a very wide power to take into account any other consideration which it deems to be relevant (but probably excluding a cost-benefit analysis, that is, of the cost to the seller in relation to the benefit to the buyer). But it must be noted that the comparison for "appropriateness" is only between the four Part 5A remedies (section 48E(3) and

(4)) and not between the chosen remedy and the common law remedies of rejection or damages. It appears from section 48E that the court has no power to substitute rejection or damages as the "appropriate" remedy which the buyer must accept. Even if the court believes that rejection or damages is an adequate remedy for the buyer, he is entitled to his chosen Part 5A remedy unless one of the other three new remedies is more "appropriate".

Choice of a traditional remedy

1–160   As is noted above, if under the previous rules of the common law or the Act the buyer is entitled to reject the goods or to claim damages ("a traditional remedy"), he is able to choose such a remedy without the court having any power to decide that one of the four Part 5A remedies is more "appropriate" and must be substituted for the buyer's chosen remedy. The only restriction on the buyer's choice of a traditional remedy is found in section 48D below, which provides that after the buyer "requires" repair or replacement he must give the seller "a reasonable time" within which to act, and may not until the expiry of that time exercise his power to reject the goods and terminate the contract for breach of condition. Apart from this restriction on his power to reject, there is no other restriction in the Act on the buyer's ability to choose either rejection or damages, despite the creation of the Part 5A remedies, though it is suggested below that the existing rules of waiver and estoppel are applicable.

Inconsistent remedies

1–161   One aspect of the relationship between the Part 5A remedies is expressly stated: section 48C (discussed above) allows reduction of price or rescission only if the buyer was not able to require repair or replacement (or, if he has done so, the seller has not provided the remedy within a reasonable time and without significant inconvenience to the buyer). It is clearly envisaged by Part 5A (*e.g.* section 48D(2)(a)) that the buyer retains the right to any remedy previously available to him before Part 5A was enacted. But any remedy sought by the buyer must not be incompatible with any remedy he has previously obtained in respect of the same lack of conformity: for example if he has obtained damages, this may preclude his attempt to require a Part 5A remedy, provided the damages were intended to cover the same aspect of non-conformity and the same "loss" as that for which the Part 5A remedy was designed. Again, termination of the contract, or rescission of the contract under section 48C will preclude a subsequent claim to specific performance or to enforcement of the requirement to repair or replace. Similarly, a requirement to repair or replace, if performed by the seller, will preclude a later rejection or rescission, but not a claim for damages for consequential loss.

Relationship of damages to the new remedies

The new Part 5A makes little attempt to integrate the new remedies   **1–162**
with the traditional ones. Apart from the restriction (discussed below, paras 1–174 *et seq.*) on rejection and termination (section 48D) Part 5A leaves it to the courts to integrate the new with the traditional remedies. In particular, nothing in Part 5A explicitly deals with the buyer's claim to damages. The issue whether repair or replacement is "disproportionate" (section 48B(3) and (4)) or "appropriate" (section 48E(3)) must be decided without reference to the availability of damages. In the result the buyer may choose a Part 5A remedy even where common law would regard damages as "adequate" (a factor that common law would regard as relevant if asked to grant an order of specific performance). The relevance of the words "disproportionate" and "appropriate" is defined by sections 48B and 48E in such a way that the only relevant comparison is with the other Part 5A remedies, and the notion of mitigation (as to which see below) is irrelevant. So, for example, even if the Part 5A remedy chosen by the buyer is disproportionate in the costs which it imposes on the seller in comparison with the damages which would be awarded to the buyer, he is free to choose that remedy. Similarly, when the court is faced with the buyer's choice of requiring the seller to repair, it may not consider awarding damages for the cost of repair by a third party (*Benjamin*, para.17–054); and when the buyer requests replacement the court may not consider awarding damages for the cost of substitute goods (*Benjamin*, para.17–055).

If the buyer has actually obtained a Part 5A remedy, any later award of damages to him must take into account the value of that remedy to him. For instance, if the buyer obtained a reduction in price under section 48C he could not later claim damages in respect of the reduction in the value of the performance he received compared with the value of the promised performance: the latter claim would have been met by the reduction in price. There may, however, be other different aspects of the buyer's loss for which damages could be recovered (see *Benjamin*, paras 17–058—17–084 for losses other than diminution in value).

Mitigation

Under the rules of mitigation (*Benjamin,* paras 16–050 *et seq.*) the   **1–163**
buyer's damages at common law must be assessed on the basis that he took reasonable steps to avoid or minimise his loss caused by the sell-

er's breach of contract. With the availability of the new remedies under Part 5A, the buyer who sues for damages for defective quality may face the question whether he should have chosen a Part 5A remedy, such as repair or replacement, because the rules of mitigation are wide enough to cover the availability of these new remedies. (He is unlikely to face a claim that he should have mitigated by choosing a reduction in the price, because even at common law the buyer's claim for damages could take account of a "price allowance" in respect of any defect in the quality of the goods: *Benjamin*, paras 17–046, 17–048, 17–052). If the buyer chooses to sue for damages instead of requiring the seller himself to repair or replace defective goods, he might be faced with the seller's allegation that he has failed to mitigate because the seller could have repaired or replaced at lower cost to himself.

Is there an order of priority among the Part 5A remedies?

1–164   The question arises as to whether (apart from "disproportionate" or "inappropriate" discussed above) there is any implicit order of priority among the Part 5A remedies. They are listed in the order given in section 48A(2)—repair, replacement, price reduction, rescission—but this does not necessarily imply an order of either choice or timing. However, the Directive (on which Part 5A was based) provided by Article 3.3 that "In the first place, the consumer may require the seller to repair the goods or he may require the seller to replace them, in either case free of charge, unless this is impossible or disproportionate". Although the words "in the first place" ("dans un premier temps") are not found in Part 5A, "cure" must be considered by the buyer before the more drastic remedies of replacement or rescission. This is confirmed by the order in which the remedies are set out, which is similar to that in the relevant provisions in the Vienna Convention. This ordering is also inherent in section 48C(2), under which, if the buyer is entitled to choose repair or replacement, he may not choose price reduction or rescission unless, having been required to do so, the seller has failed to repair or replace within a reasonable time and without significant inconvenience to the buyer. However, section 48C(2) does not place any restriction on the buyer's choice of a traditional remedy, even though rejection, or diminution or extinction of the price under section 53(1), are very similar to rescission and price reduction under Part 5A. Some ordering is found in section 48D (see below, paras 1–174—1–178) which gives the seller a reasonable time to provide a "cure"—if the buyer first requires repair, he is debarred during the "reasonable time" thereafter from rejecting the goods or requiring their replacement. Similarly, if he first requires replacement, he is debarred until a reasonable time has elapsed from either rejecting the goods or requiring their repair. But apart from section

48B(3) ("impossible" or "disproportionate") and section 48D(3) ("appropriate"), the buyer is free to choose between repair and replacement and (if the conditions in section 48C(2) are met) between price reduction and rescission.

WAIVER

The question arises as to whether any principles of waiver or estoppel **1–165** may prevent a buyer who has sought to exercise one Part 5A remedy from subsequently seeking to exercise another. This needs considering separately with respect to each remedy provided in Part 5A.

If the buyer seeks repair, but then changes his mind and seeks replace- **1–166** ment of the goods, he may not be entitled to do so if repair is the appropriate remedy, as section 48B(2) and (3) provide criteria for determining which of the two is appropriate. The same would be true if he sought replacement and subsequently changed his demand to one for repair. Part 5A appears to be drafted on the assumption that one or the other is usually appropriate. If, however, there can be a situation where either is appropriate, it is submitted that the buyer's right to change his mind must depend on whether the seller has acted in reliance on the first statement.

If the buyer seeks repair or replacement but then changes his mind **1–167** and seeks reduction of the price or rescission, his right to do so is controlled by the provisions of section 48C(2) above, under which the latter two remedies are exercisable only if he had no right to require repair or replacement at all, or if he had such a right and exercised it, but the seller has not complied timeously.

If the buyer seeks reduction of the price but then before a price **1–168** reduction is agreed changes his mind and seeks rescission, it would seem that he could do so unless the seller had acted in reliance on his indication that he was seeking a price reduction. Once the price reduction has been agreed, however, it seems that the buyer should not be able to change his mind (unless the seller consents).

If, however, the buyer indicates that he rescinds, this seems to be an **1–169** election which changes the rights of the parties, since on general principles the seller must now be released from any duty to perform further: see *Photo Production Ltd v Securicor Transport Ltd* [1980] A.C. 827, 849. The buyer could therefore change his mind and claim price reduction only with the consent of the seller.

More difficulties arise where the buyer simply does not indicate an **1–170** intention to rescind or indeed does no more than simply retain the goods for a period. At common law he may lose the right to reject by acceptance under section 35 of the Sale of Goods Act. This was considerably modified in 1994 to make the rules fairer to consumer buyers (see sections 35(2)(6) and (7), 35A: *Benjamin*, paras 12–044 *et seq.*). This section does not apply to the new provisions, since it is only made by section 11(3) of the Act applicable to a breach of condition, though there is little doubt that it would apply also to other forms of repudiatory breach. It seems necessary however to consider the policy or policies behind it to see whether they should in some way be applied across into the exercise of the new remedies. The policy or policies inherent in it are, however, not clear, or are at least mixed. The first reason for losing the right to reject, intimation of acceptance, seems to be based on the idea of election of remedies: it indicates an election not to terminate but to rely on a right to damages. This would not apply to rescission under Part 5A, which confers no right to damages; and it seems inappropriate to treat inactivity as of itself an election not to rescind but to reduce the price. The second, an act inconsistent with the ownership of the seller, created difficulties in commercial disputes in connection with resales and deliveries, difficulties now much reduced by the modification of section 35 referred to above. But many of the cases on which it was based or in which it applied referred to buyers who dealt with the goods, as by modifying them or fitting them, in a way making it impossible to return them as they were. This is a different question, and is discussed above, paras 1–149—1–150.

1–171   The third form of acceptance, retention for a reasonable time, certainly does not apply under Part 5A. It is however arguably connected with some generalised form of estoppel: see *Benjamin*, paras 12–034 *et seq.*, and it must be considered whether such reasoning would apply in this context. There is no indication in the new provisions here as to whether the buyer may lose his right to "rescind" under section 48C by indicating, or giving the impression, that he does not intend to exercise it. Where the matter is in the hands of a court, section 48E(3)(b) allows it to refuse rescission because it thinks another remedy is more appropriate; though the "other remedy" must be repair or replacement or reduction of the price—any general right to damages is not mentioned, though it is clear throughout that the changes to the Act leave the common law remedies intact. Beyond that there are no indications.

1–172   Under the general law there may be an equitable or promissory estoppel, whereby the buyer may be prevented from exercising any remedies at all because he has indicated that he is satisfied with performance as it is and will not make any claim about the breach. It is submitted that this should apply as a general legal technique for determining the equities between the parties, and is not excluded by the

Regulations and the amendments to the Sale of Goods Act which they effect. The Scottish phrase "personal bar" is worth remembering as indicating clearly that such reasoning relates to the relationship between parties and does not derive from any general regime; and the civil law knows similar reasoning under the words *venire contra factum proprium* or the notion of good faith. However, the requirements for such estoppel at common law are quite strict: the buyer must know of the facts giving rise to a right to reject and probably also that he has such a right; and there must be reliance by the seller. See *Benjamin*, para.12–035.

It may be that some other form of estoppel in the weaker form indi-   **1–173**
cated in *Panchaud Freres v Et. General Grain Co* [1970] 1 Lloyd's Rep 53, and more recently considered in *Glencore Grain Rotterdam BV v Lebanese Organisation for International Commerce* [1997] 2 Lloyd's Rep 386 (see *Benjamin*, para.12–037) could apply where a buyer by his conduct or inactivity is not to be taken to waive his rights completely, but can be taken to indicate that he did not intend to reject goods. Use has been made of such reasoning above by suggestions that sometimes a buyer cannot change his mind when the seller has acted in justifiable reliance on the assumption that the buyer was taking a particular course of action. But the cases mentioned above are commercial and this is a device developed in commercial cases. Its more generalised acceptance in a consumer case would detract considerably from the protection intended for consumers, and it may be assumed that only in a clear case would such reasoning be applied.

48D Relation to other remedies

(1) If the buyer requires the seller to repair or replace the goods the buyer   **1–174**
must not act under subsection (2) until he has given the seller a reasonable time in which to repair or replace (as the case may be) the goods.

(2) The buyer acts under this subsection if—

    (a) in England and Wales or Northern Ireland he rejects the goods and terminates the contract for breach of condition;

    (b) in Scotland he rejects any goods delivered under the contract and treats it as repudiated;

    (c) he requires the goods to be replaced or repaired (as the case may be).

INTERACTION OF THE RIGHT TO REPAIR OR REPLACEMENT AND THE COMMON LAW RIGHT TO REJECT

Many sellers in practice offer, and buyers request, repair or replace-   **1–175**
ment of defective goods. Section 35 of the Sale of Goods Act was

amended in 1994 by the insertion of section 35(6), under which "the buyer is not by virtue of this section deemed to have accepted the goods merely because—(a) he asks for, or agrees to, their repair by or under an arrangement with the seller."

1–176 Although section 35(6) is expressed in terms of requiring the buyer to give time for repair, the new section 48D continues the policy of the amendments to the 1979 Act by (in effect) permitting a buyer to require or request repair *or replacement* under Part 5A without (by doing so) losing his right to reject for breach of condition at common law. This is assumed by the requirement that he must give the seller time to repair or, as the case may be, replace the goods. It should be noted therefore that section 48D covers both repair and replacement, whereas section 35(6) only covers repair. Of course the buyers's conduct at the time may indicate acceptance in some other way, as by requesting replacement and then letting the matter lapse.

1–177 A small difficulty arises in that what the buyer is prevented from doing by section 48D is rejecting the goods and terminating the contract for *breach of condition*. If the breach is what might be called a *"Hong Kong Fir"* or "fundamental breach" (see below, para.1–199), or if there is other repudiatory conduct, he can apparently still do so without allowing the reasonable time. It may well be, however, that allowing a change of course in such circumstances would be a fair result; though equally it may have been an oversight not to cover other grounds for rejecting goods. (It may be pointed out also that the drafting of subsection (1), in so far as it refers to subsection (2)(c), appears circular, but this does not seem to be of practical significance.)

1–178 As elsewhere in the Regulations (see above, para.1–119) the words "the buyer must not act ..." give rise to difficulty. It might seem that if he does so, his act is valid though a breach of contract. It seems more likely that what is intended, though the words do not seem apt, is that if the buyer does so act, his action is simply invalid as a termination.

48E Powers of the court

1–179
(1) In any proceedings in which a remedy is sought by virtue of this Part the court, in addition to any other power it has, may act under this section.

(2) On the application of the buyer the court may make an order requiring specific performance or, in Scotland, specific implement by the seller of any obligation imposed on him by virtue of section 48B above.

(3) Subsection (4) applies if—

    (a) the buyer requires the seller to give effect to a remedy under section 48B or 48C above or has claims to rescind under section 48C, but

    (b) the court decides that another remedy under section 48B or 48C is appropriate.

(4) The court may proceed—

    (a) as if the buyer had required the seller to give effect to the other remedy, or if the other remedy is rescission under section 48C

    (b) as if the buyer had claimed to rescind the contract under that section.

(5) If the buyer has claimed to rescind the contract the court may order that any reimbursement to the buyer is reduced to take account of the use he has had of the goods since they were delivered to him.

(6) The court may make an order under this section unconditionally or on such terms and conditions as to damages, payment of the price and otherwise as it thinks just.

ENFORCEMENT BY THE COURT

The most conspicuous provision of section 48E to a common lawyer is   **1–180** that which confers powers on the court to order repair or replacement; powers which, as stated above, a common law court might well not have, or if it had them, would very rarely exercise. This provision gives express sanction to such orders, though the court has a discretion, as is indicated by the word "may" and also by the fact that common law courts in any case treat the exercise of such a power as discretionary. However, subsection (1) gives the court powers to order other remedies in any proceedings in which a remedy is sought by virtue of Part 5A, the Part at present under discussion. Not only can the court determine that repair is inappropriate and order replacement, or *vice versa*, it can also determine that reduction of the price or rescission is more appropriate than either; where the buyer claims to reduce the price, that an order for repair or replacement should be made; and correspondingly if the buyer claims rescission, that one of the other remedies should be ordered. The complex drafting of subsections (3) and (4), with its separate treatment of rescission, seems to be based on a reluctance to regard rescission as a "remedy". This leads to rescission being separately treated as a matter of drafting.

An order of specific performance to replace the non-conforming   **1–181** goods is in line with the traditional use of such an order to compel one party to a contract to perform exactly the obligation he undertook in the contract. By an order to replace, the seller is ordered to perform his original contractual obligation under the contract of sale as if his previous attempt to do so had not been made. The contract defines exactly what he must do to comply with the order. But it is an unusual use of specific performance to compel the seller to *repair*, *i.e.* to bring the goods already delivered to the buyer into conformity with the contractual description. Presumably the order to repair must be more specific than this and should inform the seller precisely what he must do to obey the order—and precisely which aspect of non-conformity must be corrected. This has always been a crucial feature of the discretionary decision to make an order of specific performance, because unlike other remedies such as damages or rejection, the sanction behind the order is quasi-criminal, in that breach of the order amounts to contempt of court. It would be strange if Part 5A was intended to give the consumer/buyer wide access to a remedy backed up by the threat of imprisonment or fine. (Even if the draftsman had used a mandatory injunction for the order to repair, this objection would still hold.)

1–182   Specific performance as a remedy in contract has always been limited by the principle that it will not be granted where damages are an adequate remedy. Under section 48E(2) and (6) an order for specific performance appears to be discretionary, but the discretion is limited by "possibility" (section 48B(3)) or by a comparison between it and the other three Part 5A remedies ("disproportionate" under section 48B(3) and (4) or "appropriate" under section 48E(3) and (4)). The discretion is therefore unable to compare the availability of damages assessed under the traditional rules as an alternative remedy to specific performance.

1–183   Two further points deserve attention. First, it may be asked whether the court may award damages in lieu of specific performance under the discretion conferred on the court by the general law found in Lord Cairns' Act 1858 (now section 50 of the Supreme Court Act 1981) (see *Benjamin*, para.17–098, n.5). It would be surprising if this route was used to circumvent the explicit provisions in Part 5A, which are to the effect that the comparison is to be made with the other Part 5A remedies.

1–184   Secondly, under section 48E(6) the order under that section may be made "unconditionally or on such terms and conditions as for damages, payment of the price and otherwise as it thinks just". The reference is not to damages awarded in lieu of an order—a free-standing award of damages—but to damages being ordered as a condition attached to an order. The corresponding power to impose conditions to an order of specific performance made under the (general) power of section 52 (*Benjamin*, paras 17–094 *et seq.*) has not been used to impose conditions on the seller, but rather on the buyer, *e.g.* to pay the price into court, or to pay a share of freight charges, or to pay interest on the price retained by the buyer pending the order (see *Benjamin*, para.17–098). It would be a novel extension of the power which refers to "damages" in section 48E(6) to interpret it to permit the court to require the *seller* to pay damages to the buyer in addition to complying with the order of specific performance, *e.g.* for some loss not remediable by compliance with the order.

It is difficult to see that a consumer buyer will often wish to have   **1–185**
recourse to obtaining a court order. It might be appropriate for a large and valuable item. It seems likely that the mere *entitlement* to these remedies may be enough to persuade the seller to replace or repair. Many sellers would do this anyway, regardless of legal requirements. It also seems that the buyer may, instead of obtaining such an order, proceed to the remedies of section 48C: see above. The obtaining of such an order would therefore be a last resort where the buyer really wanted the goods repaired or (perhaps) replaced.

48F Conformity with the contract

For the purposes of this Part, goods do not conform to a contract of sale if   **1–186**
there is, in relation to the goods, a breach of an express term of the contract or a term implied by section 13, 14 or 15 above.

MEANING OF CONFORMITY

The meaning of the phrase "conform to the contract" in section 48A is   **1–187**
here defined for United Kingdom use as involving a breach of an express term of the contract or a term implied by sections 13, 14, or 15 of the Sale of Goods Act. As to the first, express term, for rejection to be possible at common law the term would need to be a condition, or there would have to be a *Hong Kong Fir* or "fundamental" breach (see below, paras 1–197, 1–199). Under Part 5A this is not necessary, though the express term in question would presumably have to relate to conformity of the goods in a general sense. Sections 13, 14 and 15 deal with conformity with description, quality and conformity with sample and are considered in *Benjamin*, Chapter 11; section 14 on quality is slightly amended by the Regulations: see above, paras 1–063 *et seq.* Article 2.5 of the Directive specifically refers to "a shortcoming in the installation instructions" as something for which there is to be a remedy. Since supply of goods with inadequate instructions is already one of the ways in which goods may not be of satisfactory quality (see *Benjamin*, paras 11–051, 11–073) there is no specific reference to this

in the Regulations. However, the rather specific drafting of the Directive might have envisaged something more: see below, paras 1–190 *et seq.*

1–188 In fact, the Directive is initially directed only to "consumer goods". These are defined as covering "any tangible movable item" with certain exceptions (goods sold in execution, water, gas and electricity), which places little limit on them. Regulation 2 in fact adopts the wide definition of goods in section 61(1) of the Sale of Goods Act. Member States were permitted by Article 1.3 to exclude from this category second-hand goods sold at public auction where consumers have the opportunity of attending the sale in person. In the United Kingdom this was, in effect, done in a somewhat roundabout way by amending the definition of one who deals as consumer in section 12 of the Unfair Contract Terms Act 1977 so as to exclude such sales (see below, paras 1–256, 1–257). It is this definition which must be satisfied if a buyer is to benefit from the new Part 5A remedies (see section 48A(1) (a), above).

1–189 It should be noted that non-conformity with the contract in the sense of section 48F is the only basis for exercise of the new remedies, and that they do not apply to questions of right to sell, to which the existing provisions of the Act apply.

GOODS INSTALLED BY SELLER AND DEFECTIVE INSTRUCTIONS FOR INSTALLATION USED BY CONSUMER

1–190 It seems to be the intent of Article 2.5 of the Directive that defective installation by the seller or under his responsibility ranks as the sale of defective goods, and is subject to the same remedies (repair, rescission and so forth) as those for a simple sale of such goods. This is effectuated for England and Wales in the part of the Regulations dealing with conformity in connection with the contract for supply or transfer of goods, which inserts new provisions into the Supply of Goods and Services Act 1982. That is to say, such an arrangement is treated as a contract for work and materials, though the Directive in fact speaks of the installation forming "part of the contract of sale of goods". In any case, the duties imposed are in most respects almost identical. The provision achieving this result is section 11S of the 1982 Act. However, this then defines the seller's duties in such a case by reference to section 13 of the same Act, which deals not with contracts for work and materials but with the duties of a person providing services. Consonant with the general understanding of the undertakings of such a person, the duty there required is one of the exercise of reasonable care and skill only. It is very doubtful whether the Directive intended such a restricted liability in respect of installation under contracts of sale and for work and materials. See also below, para.1–241.

It also seems to be envisaged by Article 2.5 of the Directive that the **1–191** same remedies of the buyer against the seller should apply in the rather different situation where the buyer makes the installation himself, but with unsatisfactory results because the instructions are defective. It seems intended that the buyer can then call on the seller, not merely to provide better instructions, but rather to repair and so forth. This would be an entirely appropriate remedy in such a situation.

No provision in the Regulations specifically provides for this, how- **1–192** ever, and there is a difficulty in that under both the Directive and the Regulations the requirement of conformity is specifically stated as to be ascertained at the time of delivery. In the case envisaged above, the buyer is likely to install the goods after delivery, and at the time of delivery all that is wrong is that the instructions are defective, even though bad consequences follow when the buyer acts on them later. Under the existing English law, appropriate instructions are part of the requirements of satisfactory quality: see *Benjamin*, paras 11–051, 11–073. The remedy of repair or replacement in general refers to the defects existing on delivery: hence it might appear that all the buyer can do, at least initially, is require amended or better instructions. In such a case he would be better advised, if he came in time, to reject the goods at common law; or otherwise to sue for damages for loss caused by the defective instructions. But in this case, where goods become defective after delivery, though the defects in them are caused by acting on the inadequate instructions supplied with them, it can be argued that the special remedies of Part 5A are not attracted.

An alternative (and more constructive) view is that in such a case the **1–193** deficiencies in the instructions for installation or, one might add, assembly may simply lead to a breach of the implied condition of satisfactory quality of section 14(2) of the Sale of Goods Act 1979 . This would constitute a failure to conform with the contract for the purposes of the new section 48F and the buyer who deals as consumer would then be able to rely on the new Part 5A remedies in respect of all the consequences, as well as on the traditional remedies of rejection and/or damages. In the case of the Part 5A remedies it seems that the buyer can call on the seller not merely to provide better instructions, but rather to repair or replace the defective installation, provided always that this is not impossible or, as the case may be, disproportionate (see section 48B(3)).

GENERAL EFFECT OF THE NEW REGIME

1–194 If the new provisions stood alone, the effect would be that a buyer who has received non-conforming goods may require repair or replacement, and if this is not complied with may seek an order of the court for it: but this right is severely circumscribed by provisions about proportionality and appropriateness, which can be the subject of a court ruling and in any case will bring in the court's further power to designate a different one of these two remedies from that claimed, or more generally another Part 5A remedy, as more appropriate. If the right to do this is not available, or the right exists but the request has not been complied with, but not otherwise, the buyer may claim reduction of the price or rescission, apparently having unrestricted choice. If, however, he needs the assistance of a court, the court may determine that another of the remedies here discussed is more appropriate. If he does not, the question of whether estoppel principles or something like them apply to his conduct is not clear, though justice appears to demand such application in some situations. It is plain that these remedies are more complex and less incisive than the common law approach whereby the buyer may reject outright for even a comparatively small defect, though only where he comes in time. Fortunately, the common law remedies remain. The interaction of the two is further discussed in what follows (see also above, paras 1–021, 1–022).

THE EXISTING LAW CONTINUES

1–195 Nothing in the new provisions added to the Sale of Goods Act or elsewhere in the Regulations removes any of the general remedies laid down in the Act, nor detracts from those provided by the common law; and section 48D(1) above actually makes a slight modification to that law, demonstrating that the intention must be that the contractual right to reject persists. Indeed, the provisions of the 1979 Act were quite considerably modified by the Sale and Supply of Goods Act 1994 to make them more suitable to consumer disputes, as by reformulating the name and definition of the general quality provision in section 14(2) ("satisfactory quality") and substantially modifying the rules on acceptance (see *Benjamin*, paras 12–044 *et seq.*). As now formulated, the remedies outside Part 5A are in many respects more favourable to the consumer than the romanistic solutions added by sections 48A-C, and it was therefore highly appropriate to conserve them rather than replace them entirely with new and unfamiliar techniques which are in some ways less favourable to consumers. The consequent interaction of the general law with the new provisions presents, however, even more problems for the adviser of consumers than do some of the situations under the new provisions alone.

THE EXISTING LAW

This is considered in Chapter 11 of *Benjamin*. It may be loosely sum-   **1–196**
marised as follows. There are two remedies only: rejection, and in
general, termination of the contract *ex nunc*, together with damages
for additional losses suffered despite termination; and damages only.
Damages are limited by the common law rules as to remoteness,
under which only loss that is to be regarded as having been in the
contemplation of the parties when the contract was made is recoverable, and as to mitigation of loss.

Whether or not the buyer can reject the goods depends first on   **1–197**
whether the promise which the seller has broken is a condition or a
warranty. A condition is a term with which exact compliance is
required, any breach of which, however slight, and whether or not this
is in the actual situation of concern to the buyer, entitles the buyer to
reject the goods unless he has accepted them, *i.e.* is too late to do so.
The rejection of the goods is normally associated with the right to
terminate the contract altogether (treat it as discharged) and buy elsewhere, though there may be situations where the seller can make a
second tender of conforming goods. That the consumer too can often
demand this is indeed the purpose of section 48B. But in general, the
delivery of non-conforming goods may be assumed to destroy the confidence of the buyer and hence also be repudiatory conduct by the
seller, entitling the buyer to terminate the contract. The question of
quantitative deficiency is separately dealt with but the results are
likely to be the same: see *Benjamin*, paras 8 044 *et seq*.

A contract term of less significance is called a warranty, and only gives   **1–198**
rise to a right to damages, subject to what is said below.

The buyer also has the right, independently of the Act, to terminate   **1–199**
the contract if the nature and effects of the breach are such as to
deprive him of substantially the whole benefit of the contract—the
so-called *Hong Kong Fir* or "fundamental", breach which has been
held to apply to contracts for the sale of goods though not mentioned
in the Act (see *Benjamin*, paras 10–033 *et seq.*, 12–023); and a breach
of warranty, or an aggregation of breaches of warranty, may probably
have this effect sometimes. He also has that right, as is foreshadowed
above, if the conduct of the seller is repudiatory of his obligations; and
this also exists though not directly mentioned in the Act: see *Benjamin*, para.12–019.

In the present context the basic duties of conformity are laid down by   **1–200**
sections 13, 14 and 15 of the Act as conditions, and there can also be
express conditions as to conformity. The result is that the buyer can

normally reject on the basis of breach of condition alone without rely-
ing on either of the other two techniques referred to above. This right
is a strict one: there is no specific seller's right to cure, nor buyer's right
to demand it. Informal proposals for a cure regime were rejected by
the Law Commission in 1987 as inappropriately reducing the consumer's power of outright rejection of unsatisfactory goods.

1–201   The right to reject is however lost in accordance with the provisions of
section 35 of the Act when the buyer intimates acceptance, or does an
act inconsistent with the seller's ownership, or, most important in this
context, where after a lapse of a reasonable time he retains them without intimating to the seller that he has rejected them. Although section 35 was, as stated above, considerably amended in 1994 to
eliminate acceptance in certain situations, principally those where the
buyer has no opportunity of examining the goods or asks for or agrees
to repair, it has been generally assumed that the drastic right to reject
is lost in a comparatively short time. This view was largely based on a
first instance decision on the unamended wording of section 35, *Bernstein v Pamson Motors (Golders Green) Ltd* [1987] 2 All E.R. 220, in
which the right to reject a car was lost in a month, though the buyer
was elderly and did not use it much and the defect manifested itself in
winter, when the car was used even less than normal (also the buyer
was unwell for part of the time). The test applied was one of "a reasonable practical interval in commercial terms" (at p.230). There were at
the time strong views expressed in the retail trade that a short-term
right to reject was appropriate.

1–202   However, a recent decision of the Court of Appeal, *Clegg v Olle
Andersson* [2003] EWCA Civ 320, [2003] 2 Lloyd's Rep. 32, indicates
that the matter should no longer be so viewed now that appropriate
amendments have been made to section 35. It is said that the test
applied in *Bernstein* does not represent the law since the statutory
changes of 1994; and the right to reject a yacht after eight months was
affirmed. The case does not, however, give much guidance beyond
this, and is also based on rather special facts: not many consumers buy
yachts. So, although it certainly relaxes the notion of "reasonable
time" somewhat, it should not be assumed that the common law right
to reject lasts as long as the remedies under Part 5A, even if these had
been limited (as they are not, though the Directive envisaged it) to
two years (see below, paras 1–214 *et seq.*). For examples of older case
law on acceptance, which may sometimes be useful, see *Benjamin*,
para.12–055.

1–203   Where the buyer justifiably rejects he may normally recover the whole
price on the basis of total failure of consideration. The provisions of
sections 48C(3) and 48F(5), above, allowing deduction for use only
apply to the new statutory remedies: they do not affect the general

law. Nor does the power conferred on the court by section 48E to award one remedy instead of another apply to the general law: it is again limited to cases where a remedy is sought "by virtue of this Part".

CHANGE TO THE EXISTING LAW

Section 48D(1) (above) provides that if the buyer has under the new **1–204** provisions required repair or replacement, he must not (in effect) revert to the common law right of rejection until he has given the seller a reasonable opportunity to comply. This defers the operation of section 35.

INTERACTION OF NEW REMEDIES WITH THE EXISTING LAW

If one now considers how a dissatisfied consumer who can establish a **1–205** breach of the conformity requirements of sections 13, 14 or 15 of the Sale of Goods Act or of an express term relating to conformity, can proceed on the basis of both these sets of remedies the answer appears to be as follows.

If he can establish that the goods were non-conforming on delivery **1–206** (the rules for which are fairly strict in his favour, though not as strict as they are in commercial cases where there are contract specifications) he can reject them at common law if he comes in time; and the previous assumption that this must be done quickly may have been overstressed. He can also sue for damages. He must however establish the non-conformity himself: he is not entitled to the benefit of the sixmonth presumption of section 48A(3), since this only relates to the "new" remedies created by Part 5A. It only applies "for the purposes of subsection (1)(b) above" and subsection (1)(b) is part of the designation of when the "new" remedies apply. Subject to this point the common law remedies seem so far superior.

The consumer buyer can instead proceed under the new provisions by **1–207** requiring repair or replacement while initially retaining his common law rights (see section 48D(1) above) if the circumstances under which this can be required in section 48B apply. Many buyers must in effect do this already, and sellers cooperate without the need for a legal right. If he does not secure this, he could if he wished take proceedings under it to enforce the right, though the result of these might be unpredictable. But the inference from section 48D(1) is that he can instead revert to his common law rights, reject the goods and terminate the contract. It must be assumed that the running of the "reasonable time" for the purposes of the common law notion of acceptance (section 35 of the Sale of Goods Act) is suspended pending the statutory rights being exercised. Section 35(6) provides that the buyer does not accept the goods merely because he asks for or agrees to their repair, but it must surely now be inferred that the same applies if he seeks replacement.

1–208   The *seller* has no right to demand to repair or replace, though as stated above, he may in practice point out to the buyer that if he does not permit repair or replacement he may lose the prospect of exercising his other rights under Part 5A to price reduction or rescission. If the buyer sues for damages only, he may sometimes find that the court holds that he ought to have mitigated his loss by accepting the offer to cure: see *The Solholt* [1983] 1 Lloyd's Rep.605; *Benjamin*, paras 16–050 *et seq*.

1–209   The buyer may, instead of proceeding under the common law rules, proceed under Part 5A. The new provisions give him the benefit of the six-month presumption where this is applicable. However, where repair or replacement are possible and not disproportionate to each other, or to the remedies of reduction of the price and rescission, he must have demanded such repair or replacement (if it was appropriate) to retain the possibility of eventual rescission (rejection) or reduction of the price. If repair or replacement is offered he has no such right unless the offer is not made good.

1–210   If the buyer gives an opportunity for repair or replacement and it does not occur, he may, as stated above, revert to the common law position and reject the goods unless he is caught by one of the provisions of section 35, particularly the "reasonable time" provision. But otherwise, he may continue with the Part 5A regime by seeking reduction of the price or rescission (termination) at his choice, and, as explained in para.1–215 below, the right to rescind may here persist for a considerable period. If, however, he needs the assistance of the court there is again a danger that a court may then find some other Part 5A remedy more appropriate (which would not be true at common law). The most "dangerous" of these to a person versed in the common law approach is reduction of the price, which may, at least in theory, be imposed on a buyer whose only desire is to get rid of the goods and buy again. Furthermore, if he seeks to rescind and get his money back he may be compelled to make an allowance for the use which he has had of the goods in the interim, which is not true at common law. However, it would appear that the right to damages at common law persists in respect of special or consequential losses.

All the above will prove difficult to apply in practice, especially   **1–211**
because (except in the case of an unusually well-advised buyer) these
possible causes of action will often be used only to form the basis for
an *ex post facto* explanation of much of the seller's conduct. In general
the Part 5A remedies, which may seem more diverse and to offer more
choice, are heavily regulated by matters of proportionality, reasonableness and the like, which in the case of dispute may require deter-
mination, usually retrospectively, by a court.

Overall, the common law right to reject requires no preliminaries and   **1–212**
hence is more effective if exercised quickly. It will not be lost even if
repair or replacement is demanded, but if that is not forthcoming it
may be lost quite soon. The Part 5A remedy of rescission has the
advantage of the six-month presumption, and can go on for longer
than the common law right (see below), but is hedged around with
statutory controls as to what is appropriate, which may prove difficult
to apply. Hence a buyer who can prove that the goods do not conform
on delivery may reject immediately or fairly soon thereafter, and may
first request repair or replacement without losing this advantage. He
must, however, consider repair or replacement if he wishes to be able
to have a legal right to reduce the price, or to have the benefit of a
longer-lasting right to rescind accompanied by the six-month
presumption.

It is suggested above that if the sale is by instalments, the buyer seeks   **1–213**
to reject in part, or the defect is quantitative, the United Kingdom
buyer would do better to rely on the existing law, because of the
uncertainty of the position under the "rescission" remedy of section
48C. The general law as to repudiatory breach is likely to be needed in
the background because the Regulations do not, as the Directive did
not, provide for the coexistence of rules as to "fundamental breach"
found in the Vienna Convention.

TIME LIMITS FOR THE CONSUMER'S REMEDIES

Exercise of rights such as those provided by the new Part 5A are fre-   **1–214**
quently in romanistic systems subjected to a flat time bar, for example,
two years. The acceptability of such time bars derives from the
Roman law limitations, under which the *actio redhibitoria* could only
be brought within six months, and the *actio quanti minoris* within one
year. Article 5.1 of the Directive requires Member States to give effect
to such rights where the lack of conformity becomes apparent within
two years of delivery. It also allows Member States to require that
notice be given within two months of the discovery of the lack of
conformity.

1–215   This technique is not used in common law, which relies instead on the less precise but more flexible notion of acceptance. Hence to provide for a two-year time limit, even on the rights introduced under the Regulations, would often reduce the overall protection of the buyer under common law, and certainly make it more complicated. Such a suggestion was rejected by the Law Commission in 1987 largely on the ground that a single time limit is inappropriate to the many types of goods that may be the subject of sale: see Law Com No. 160, Scot. Law Com No. 104, paras 5.15–5.19. The Regulations therefore introduce no such limit, and *a fortiori* do not impose the two-month restriction for giving notice. The result is that all these remedies can in English law be exercised without formal limit of time, save that where an action in court is required it may be barred after the normal limitation period of six years. This doubtless far exceeds what was envisaged by the Directive, which is based on different presuppositions.

1–216   Article 7.2 of the Directive allows Member States to provide that shorter periods may be agreed between buyer and seller in the case of second-hand goods. Since the longer period itself was not adopted, this concession has not been adopted either.

1–217   When the 1994 amendments of the Sale of Goods Act were considered, there was pressure from consumer interests for a "long term right to reject" of long-lasting items such as washing machines, which might go wrong after several years by reason of a deficiency inherent at the time of delivery. This was to some extent met by the addition of a reference to "durability" in the guidelines for the test of satisfactory quality. But the power of rejection after a considerable period was still unlikely by reason of the acceptance provisions as then understood. The idea of changing this was rejected: see Law Com. No. 160, Scot. Law Com No. 104 (1987), paras 5.6 to 5.9, as potentially unfair on sellers, and on the ground that an efficient right to reject within a short period of time was more desirable than a doubtful right to reject over a longer period.

1–218   The new remedies are plainly envisaged by the Directive as having their own time limit of at least two years to deal with the problem. But the non-application of such a time limit in the United Kingdom means that the right to rescind under section 48C, being not limited by the acceptance provisions of section 35, could in theory be open forever number unless the assistance of a court was required, in which case it could only continue for the normal period under the Limitation Act of six years. Official explanations of the new provisions suggest that *all* rights end after six years, but although this may be so in practice it can only legally be correct for the exercise of judicial procedures. Exactly how this will work is difficult to envisage: the right to rescind is hedged around with restrictions based on proportionality and appropriateness which will solve most cases in practice. But the omission of any time limit certainly extends the period during which the right to rescind may be exercised beyond what exists for rejection under the common law, and may create something near to the "long term right to reject" which it was decided not to adopt in 1987. This effect is to some extent counterbalanced by the increasing difficulty (the later the attempt to rescind) of proving that the defect inhered at the time of delivery and has not been caused by general wear and tear, misuse and so forth. It must be remembered that the presumption in the buyer's favour referred to above only lasts for six months.

CONTRACTING OUT OF PART 5A

Virtually the whole of the Sale of Goods Act is facultative and not   **1–219**
mandatory. Hence there would appear to be nothing in the Act to prevent a contract whereby the buyer contracted out of his rights under sections 48A to 48F completely. However, a clause to this effect is likely to be caught by unfair contract terms legislation. In particular, where the buyer deals as consumer within the meaning of the Unfair Contract Terms Act 1977 any exclusion or restriction of liability for breach of the obligations arising from sections 13, 14 and 15 of the Sale of Goods Act is ineffective: see *Benjamin*, para.13–076. Section 13(1) of the 1977 Act states that where the Act prevents exclusion or restriction of any liability it also prevents "excluding or restricting any right or remedy in respect of the liability." Though the new Part 5A remedies had not been introduced into the Sale of Goods Act when the Unfair Contract Terms Act came into effect, it seems correct that the new rights should be regarded as protected by this provision. Such indeed is required by Article 7.1 of the Directive.

If this were not so, such exclusions might instead be tested by refer-   **1–220**
ence to section 3(1) of the Unfair Contract Terms Act itself, which subjects to a test of reasonableness clauses excluding or restricting liability in respect of a breach of contract when one party deals as consumer. They might also be caught by the Unfair Terms in Consumer Contracts Regulations 1999 (SI 1999/2083), which cover contract terms that "contrary to the requirement of good faith ... [cause] a significant imbalance in the parties' rights and obligations arising under [the contract] to the detriment of the consumer." In either case, it might be thought that an exclusion of Part 5A in whole or in part might be reasonable, for it would be difficult to say that the overall English position prior to the enactment of Part 5A was unreasonable

or prejudicial to the consumer. As noted above, it was and is in most respects more favourable to the consumer. Section 6 of the Unfair Contract Terms Act however pre-empts this question. See further above, paras 1–035 *et seq.*

1–221   The above concerns exclusion of the new remedies. An exclusion of the six-month presumption of section 48A(3), on the other hand, is plainly prejudicial to the consumer and would probably be caught by both the latter two provisions above; and a clause which, by wide wording, took in exclusion of this provision could well be wholly ineffective (see *Benjamin*, para.13–080). But such an exclusion is probably also caught by section 13(1) of the Unfair Contract Terms Act on the basis that it "exclude[s] rules of evidence or procedure". Hence it is again completely ineffective under section 6 of that Act. Special rules apply to public auctions of second-hand goods: see below, paras 1–256, 1–257.

1–222   Finally, the following diagram is offered as an aid to understanding the new Part 5A remedies and their complex relationship to the traditional remedies.

The consumer's remedies after the Sale and Supply of Goods to Consumer Regulations 2002

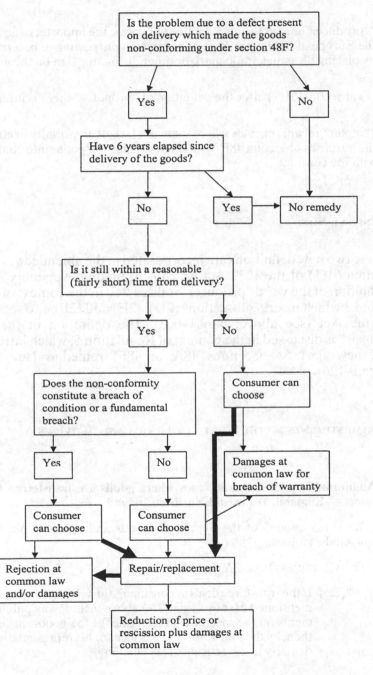

Other amendments to the 1979 Act

1-224   **6.**—(1) In section 61(1) after the definition of "plaintiff" there is inserted—

""producer" means the manufacturer of goods, the importer of goods into the European Economic Area or any person purporting to be a producer by placing his name, trade mark or other distinctive sign on the goods;";

(2) in section 61(1) after the definition of "property" there is inserted—

""repair" means, in cases where there is a lack of conformity in goods for the purposes of section 48F of this Act, to bring the goods into conformity with the contract;".

GENERAL NOTE

1-225   These two new definitions are incorporated in the amended version of section 61(1) of the 1979 Act which is printed as Appendix A. The definition of the word "producer" is discussed in the context of Regulation 3 which inserts subsections (2D), (2E) and (2F) into section 14 of the Act (see above, para.1–068). The definition of the word "repair" is discussed in the context of Regulation 5, which introduces the new Part 5A (sections 48A to 48F) remedies (see above, para.1–126).

AMENDMENTS TO THE SUPPLY OF GOODS AND SERVICES ACT 1982

Additional implied terms in cases where goods are transferred to consumers—England, Wales and Northern Ireland

1-226   **7.**—(1) Section 4 of the Supply of Goods and Services Act 1982 is amended as follows.

(2) After subsection (2A) insert—

"(2B) If the transferee deals as consumer, the relevant circumstances mentioned in subsection (2A) above include any public statements on the specific characteristics of the goods made about them by the transferor, the producer or his representative, particularly in advertising or on labelling.

(2C) A public statement is not by virtue of subsection (2B) above a relevant circumstance for the purposes of subsection (2A) above in the case of a contract for the transfer of goods, if the transferor shows that—

(a) at the time the contract was made, he was not, and could not reasonably have been, aware of the statement,

(b) before the contract was made, the statement had been withdrawn in public or, to the extent that it contained anything which was incorrect or misleading, it had been corrected in public, or

(c) the decision to acquire the goods could not have been influenced by the statement.

(2D) Subsections (2B) and (2C) above do not prevent any public statement from being a relevant circumstance for the purposes of subsection (2A) above (whether or not the transferee deals as consumer) if the statement would have been such a circumstance apart from those subsections.".

GENERAL NOTE

Regulation 7 amends section 4 of the Supply of Goods and Services   **1–227**
Act 1982 in a way which is identical in all material respects to the amendments to section 14 of the Sale of Goods Act 1979 which are introduced by Regulation 3 and commented on above (see paras 1–063 *et seq.*). The relevant contracts which are affected are those which fall within the scope of Part I of the 1982 Act. Section 1 of the 1982 Act provides that such contracts are ones under which one person transfers or agrees to transfer the property in goods, other than an excepted contract. By section 1(2) "an excepted contract means any of the following—(a) a contract of sale of goods; (b) a hire purchase agreement; (c) a contract under which the property in goods is (or is to be) transferred in exchange for trading stamps on their redemption; (d) a transfer or agreement to transfer which is made by deed and for which there is no consideration other than the presumed consideration imported by the deed; (e) a contract intended to operate by way of mortgage, pledge, charge or other security." Section 1(3) adds that a contract is a contract for the transfer of goods whether or not services are also provided or to be provided under the contract and, subject to section 1(2), whatever is the nature of the consideration for the transfer or agreement to transfer. The main concern is therefore with contracts for work and materials and contracts of exchange or barter. For discussion of the general nature of such contracts, see *Benjamin*, paras 1–041—1–042 and 1–034—1–039).

Additional implied terms in cases where goods are transferred to consumers—Scotland

1–228   **8.**—(1) Section 11D of the Supply of Goods and Services Act 1982 is amended as follows.

(2) After subsection (3) insert—

"(3A) If the contract for the transfer of goods is a consumer contract, the relevant circumstances mentioned in subsection (3) above include any public statements on the specific characteristics of the goods made about them by the transferor, the producer or his representative, particularly in advertising or on labelling.

(3B) A public statement is not by virtue of subsection (3A) above a relevant circumstance for the purposes of subsection (3) above in the case of a contract for the transfer of goods, if the transferor shows that—

(a) at the time the contract was made, he was not, and could not reasonably have been, aware of the statement,

(b) before the contract was made, the statement had been withdrawn in public or, to the extent that it contained anything which was incorrect or misleading, it had been corrected in public, or

(c) the decision to acquire the goods could not have been influenced by the statement.

(3C) Subsections (3A) and (3B) above do not prevent any public statement from being a relevant circumstance for the purposes of subsection (3) above (whether or not the contract for the transfer of goods is a consumer contract) if the statement would have been such a circumstance apart from those subsections."

(3) After subsection (9) insert—

"(10) For the purposes of this section, "consumer contract" has the same meaning as in section 11F(3) below."

GENERAL NOTE

1–229 Regulation 8, which applies to Scotland only, amends section 11D of the Supply of Goods and Services Act 1982 and is the equivalent of Regulation 7, above, which applies to England, Wales and Northern Ireland.

Transferee's additional remedies in consumer cases

1–230   **9.**—(1) After Part 1A of the Supply of Goods and Services Act 1982 insert—

"PART 1B

ADDITIONAL RIGHTS OF TRANSFEREE IN CONSUMER CASES

11M Introductory

(1) This section applies if—   **1–231**

    (a) the transferee deals as consumer or, in Scotland, there is a consumer contract in which the transferee is a consumer, and

    (b) the goods do not conform to the contract for the transfer of goods at the time of delivery.

(2) If this section applies, the transferee has the right—

    (a) under and in accordance with section 11N below, to require the transferor to repair or replace the goods, or

    (b) under and in accordance with section 11P below—

        (i) to require the transferor to reduce the amount to be paid for the transfer by the transferee by an appropriate amount, or

        (ii) to rescind the contract with regard to the goods in question.

(3) For the purposes of subsection (1)(b) above, goods which do not conform to the contract for the transfer of goods at any time within the period of six months starting with the date on which the goods were delivered to the transferee must be taken not to have so conformed at that date.

(4) Subsection (3) above does not apply if—

    (a) it is established that the goods did so conform at that date;

    (b) its application is incompatible with the nature of the goods or the nature of the lack of conformity.

(5) For the purposes of this section, "consumer contract" has the same meaning as in section 11F(3) above.

11N Repair or replacement of the goods

(1) If section 11M above applies, the transferee may require the   **1–232**
transferor—

    (a) to repair the goods, or

    (b) to replace the goods.

(2) If the transferee requires the transferor to repair or replace the goods, the transferor must—

(a) repair or, as the case may be, replace the goods within a reasonable time but without causing significant inconvenience to the transferee;

(b) bear any necessary costs incurred in doing so (including in particular the cost of any labour, materials or postage).

(3) The transferee must not require the transferor to repair or, as the case may be, replace the goods if that remedy is—

(a) impossible,

(b) disproportionate in comparison to the other of those remedies, or

(c) disproportionate in comparison to an appropriate reduction in the purchase price under paragraph (a), or rescission under paragraph (b), of section 11P(1) below.

(4) One remedy is disproportionate in comparison to the other if the one imposes costs on the transferor which, in comparison to those imposed on him by the other, are unreasonable, taking into account—

(a) the value which the goods would have if they conformed to the contract for the transfer of goods,

(b) the significance of the lack of conformity to the contract for the transfer of goods, and

(c) whether the other remedy could be effected without significant inconvenience to the transferee.

(5) Any question as to what is a reasonable time or significant inconvenience is to be determined by reference to—

(a) the nature of the goods, and

(b) the purpose for which the goods were acquired.

11P Reduction of purchase price or rescission of contract

1–233   (1) If section 11M above applies, the transferee may—

(a) require the transferor to reduce the purchase price of the goods in question to the transferee by an appropriate amount, or

(b) rescind the contract with regard to those goods,

if the condition in subsection (2) below is satisfied.

(2) The condition is that—

(a) by virtue of section 11N(3) above the transferee may require neither repair nor replacement of the goods, or

(b) the transferee has required the transferor to repair or replace the goods, but the transferor is in breach of the requirement of section 11N(2)(a) above to do so within a reasonable time and without significant inconvenience to the transferee.

(3) If the transferee rescinds the contract, any reimbursement to the transferee may be reduced to take account of the use he has had of the goods since they were delivered to him.

11Q Relation to other remedies etc.

(1) If the transferee requires the transferor to repair or replace the goods the transferee must not act under subsection (2) until he has given the transferor a reasonable time in which to repair or replace (as the case may be) the goods.   **1–234**

(2) The transferee acts under this subsection if—

    (a) in England and Wales or Northern Ireland he rejects the goods and terminates the contract for breach of condition;

    (b) in Scotland he rejects any goods delivered under the contract and treats it as repudiated; or

    (c) he requires the goods to be replaced or repaired (as the case may be).

11R Powers of the court

(1) In any proceedings in which a remedy is sought by virtue of this Part the court, in addition to any other power it has, may act under this section.   **1–235**

(2) On the application of the transferee the court may make an order requiring specific performance or, in Scotland, specific implement by the transferor of any obligation imposed on him by virtue of section 11N above.

(3) Subsection (4) applies if—

    (a) the transferee requires the transferor to give effect to a remedy under section 11N or 11P above or has claims to rescind under section 11P, but

    (b) the court decides that another remedy under section 11N or 11P is appropriate.

(4) The court may proceed—

    (a) as if the transferee had required the transferor to give effect to the other remedy, or if the other remedy is rescission under section 11P,

    (b) as if the transferee had claimed to rescind the contract under that section.

(5) If the transferee has claimed to rescind the contract the court may order that any reimbursement to the transferee is reduced to take account of the use he has had of the goods since they were delivered to him.

(6) The court may make an order under this section unconditionally or on such terms and conditions as to damages, payment of the price and otherwise as it thinks just.

11S Conformity with the contract

1–236

(1) Goods do not conform to a contract for the supply or transfer of goods if—

(a) there is, in relation to the goods, a breach of an express term of the contract or a term implied by section 3, 4 or 5 above or, in Scotland, by section 11C, 11D or 11E above, or

(b) installation of the goods forms part of the contract for the transfer of goods, and the goods were installed by the transferor, or under his responsibility, in breach of the term implied by section 13 below or (in Scotland) in breach of any term implied by any rule of law as to the manner in which the installation is carried out."

GENERAL NOTE

1–237 Regulation 9 adds a new Part 1B (sections 11M to 11S) headed "Additional Rights of Transferee in Consumer Cases" to the Supply of Goods and Services Act 1982. As is explained in the General Note to Regulation 7, above (see para.1–227), the relevant contracts to which these additional rights apply are those which fall within the scope of Part I of the 1982 Act and which are defined in section 1 of that Act. Broadly speaking, these are contracts for work and materials and contracts of exchange or barter, but not contracts of hire or hire-purchase.

1–238 Regulation 9 (Part 1B) was, it seems, included in the Regulations pursuant to the interpretation which the Department of Trade and Industry had placed on Article 1.4 of the Directive. As has already been noted (see above, para.1–010), this was that it extended the scope of the Directive beyond contracts for the sale of goods to include what in English law would be called contracts for work and materials. When allowance is made for the variations in terminology associated with the differing nature of the transactions ("transferee", as opposed to "buyer" etc.), the wording of Part 1B mirrors that of the new Part 5A (sections 48A to 48F) of the Sale of Goods Act which was commented on in detail above (see para.1–095 *et seq.*). In fact, apart from the differences between the new sections 48F and 11S to which reference is made below (see para.1–241), the only other difference appears to be that whereas sections 48C(3) and 48F are expressed as applying 'For the purposes of this Part' (that is, Part 5A), the equivalent provisions in sections 11P(3) and 11S omit these words. By way of contrast, the words are included in section 11R(1) which is the equivalent of section 48E(1). The matter does not appear to carry any significance.

In view of the close equivalence between Part 1B of the 1982 Act and   **1–239**
Part 5A of the 1979 Act, it is not proposed to consider the scheme of remedies under Part 1B as such. However, attention should be drawn to one important distinction between contracts for the sale of goods and other transactions. This is that contracts which fall outside the scope of the 1979 Act do not have an equivalent of the provisions as to acceptance of section 35 of that Act. The loss of the right to reject non-conforming goods is governed, rather, by common law principles, including those of affirmation and waiver.

To generalise, it may be said that these principles are more favourable   **1–240**
to the transferee than the provisions of the 1979 Act. In particular, it seems that the transferee will not be taken to have elected to affirm the contract unless, in the words of Lord Denning, M.R., "he knows of the defects and by his conduct elects to go on with the contract despite them" (see *Farnworth Finance Facilities Ltd* v *Attryde* [1970] 1 W.L.R. 1053, 1059). Affirmation may be implied as well as express, for example by pressing for the performance of the contract. However, mere inactivity and the passage of time after discovering the breach will not, of itself, constitute affirmation unless the other party is prejudiced by the delay or the delay is such as to constitute evidence of a decision to affirm: see generally *Allen* v *Robles* [1969] 1 W.L.R. 1193; also *Peyman* v *Lanjani* [1985] Ch.457; *Moore Large & Co Ltd* v *Hermes Credit and Guarantee Plc* [2003] 1 Lloyd's Rep. 163, 179–180. In this, the general common law principles are to be contrasted with the provisions of section 35(4) of the 1979 Act whereby the right to reject may be lost by the lapse of a reasonable period of time (see above, paras 1–170 *et seq.*) and, in general, *Benjamin*, paras 12–035—12–037).

Conformity with the Contract

Section 11S(1)(a) of the 1982 Act is the equivalent of section 48F of   **1–241**
the 1979 Act which is discussed above (see above, paras 1–186 *et seq.*). As is apparent, it defines non-conformity by reference to a breach of an express term of the contract or a term implied by sections 3 (correspondence with description), 4 (satisfactory quality and reasonable fitness for specified purposes) and 5 (correspondence with sample). Section 11S(1)(b) seeks to implement the first sentence of Article 2.5 of the Directive which states that: "Any lack of conformity resulting from incorrect installation of the consumer goods shall be deemed to

be equivalent to lack of conformity of the goods if installation forms part of the contract of sale of the goods and the goods were installed by the seller or under his responsibility." As has been observed above when discussing the new Part 5A remedies of the Sale of Goods Act (see paras 1–012, 1–190), the reference in section 11S(1)(b) to section 13 of the 1982 Act is a reference to an obligation to exercise reasonable care and skill only. This raises an issue of probable non-compliance with the Directive, since Article 2.5 appears to envisage a strict obligation to install correctly.

Additional implied terms where goods are hired to consumers—England, Wales and Northern Ireland

1–242   **10.**—(1) Section 9 of the Supply of Goods and Services Act 1982 is amended as follows.

(2) After subsection (2A) insert—

"(2B) If the bailee deals as consumer, the relevant circumstances mentioned in subsection (2A) above include any public statements on the specific characteristics of the goods made about them by the bailor, the producer or his representative, particularly in advertising or on labelling.

(2C) A public statement is not by virtue of subsection (2B) above a relevant circumstance for the purposes of subsection (2A) above in the case of a contract for the hire of goods, if the bailor shows that—

(a) at the time the contract was made, he was not, and could not reasonably have been, aware of the statement,
(b) before the contract was made, the statement had been withdrawn in public or, to the extent that it contained anything which was incorrect or misleading, it had been corrected in public, or
(c) the decision to acquire the goods could not have been influenced by the statement.

(2D) Subsections (2B) and (2C) above do not prevent any public statement from being a relevant circumstance for the purposes of subsection (2A) above (whether or not the bailee deals as consumer) if the statement would have been such a circumstance apart from those subsections."

GENERAL NOTE

1–243   Regulation 10 amends section 9 of the Supply of Goods and Services Act 1982 in a way which is identical in all material respects to the amendments to section 14 of the Sale of Goods Act 1979 which are introduced by Regulation 3 and commented on above (see paras

1–063 *et seq.*). The relevant contracts which are affected are as indicated in section 6(1) of the 1982 Act, namely contracts for the hire of goods, which are defined to mean contracts "under which one person bails or agrees to bail goods to another by way of hire, other than an excepted contract." By section 6(2) an excepted contract means "(a) a hire-purchase agreement; (b) a contract under which goods are (or are to be) bailed in exchange for trading stamps on their redemption." As in the case of the amendments to section 4 of the 1982 Act (see above, paras 1–226—1–227), section 6(3) adds that a contract is a contract for the hire of goods, whether or not services are also provided or to be provided under the contract, and, subject to section 6(2), whatever is the nature of the consideration for the bailment or agreement to bail by way of hire.

Additional implied terms where goods are hired to consumers—Scotland

11.—(1) Section 11J of the Supply of Goods and Services Act 1982 is amended as follows.   **1–244**

(2) After subsection (3) insert—

"(3A) If the contract for the hire of goods is a consumer contract, the relevant circumstances mentioned in subsection (3) above include any public statements on the specific characteristics of the goods made about them by the hirer, the producer or his representative, particularly in advertising or on labelling.

(3B) A public statement is not by virtue of subsection (3A) above a relevant circumstance for the purposes of subsection (3) above in the case of a contract for the hire of goods, if the hirer shows that—

(a) at the time the contract was made, he was not, and could not reasonably have been, aware of the statement,

(b) by the time the contract was made, the statement had been withdrawn in public or, to the extent that it contained anything which was incorrect or misleading, it had been corrected in public, or

(c) the decision to acquire the goods could not have been influenced by the statement.

(3C) Subsections (3A) and (3B) above do not prevent any public statement from being a relevant circumstance for the purposes of subsection (3) above (whether or not the contract for the hire of goods is a consumer contract) if the statement would have been such a circumstance apart from those subsections.".

(3) At the end of the section add—

"(10) For the purposes of this section, "consumer contract" has the same meaning as in section 11F(3) above.".

GENERAL NOTE

1–245   Regulation 11, which applies to Scotland only, amends section 11J of the Supply of Goods and Services Act 1982 and is the equivalent of Regulation 10 above, which applies to England, Wales and Northern Ireland.

Other Amendments to 1982 Act

1–246   **12.**—(1) In section 18(1) after the definition of "hire purchase agreement" there is inserted—

""producer" means the manufacturer of goods, the importer of goods into the European Economic Area or any person purporting to be a producer by placing his name, trade mark or other distinctive sign on the goods;".

(2) In section 18(1) after the definition of "redemption" there is inserted—

""repair" means, in cases where there is a lack of conformity in goods for the purposes of this Act, to bring the goods into conformity with the contract."

GENERAL NOTE

1–247   These two definitions are the same as those introduced by Regulation 6 into section 61(1) of the Sale of Goods Act 1979 (see above, para.1–224).

AMENDMENTS TO THE SUPPLY OF GOODS (IMPLIED TERMS) ACT 1973

Additional implied terms in consumer cases

1–248   **13.**—(1) Section 10 of the Supply of Goods (Implied Terms) Act 1973 is amended as follows.

(2) After subsection (2C) insert—

"(2D) If the person to whom the goods are bailed or hired deals as consumer or, in Scotland, if the goods are hired to a person under a consumer contract, the relevant circumstances mentioned in subsection (2A) above include any public statements on the specific characteristics of the goods made about them by the creditor, the producer or his representative, particularly in advertising or on labelling.

(2E) A public statement is not by virtue of subsection (2D) above a relevant circumstance for the purposes of subsection (2A) above in the case of a contract of hire-purchase, if the creditor shows that—

(a) at the time the contract was made, he was not, and could not reasonably have been, aware of the statement,

(b) before the contract was made, the statement had been withdrawn in public or, to the extent that it contained anything which was incorrect or misleading, it had been corrected in public, or

(c) the decision to acquire the goods could not have been influenced by the statement.

(2F) Subsections (2D) and (2E) above do not prevent any public statement from being a relevant circumstance for the purposes of subsection (2A) above (whether or not the person to whom the goods are bailed or hired deals as consumer or, in Scotland, whether or not the goods are hired to a person under a consumer contract) if the statement would have been such a circumstance apart from those subsections."

(3) At the end of the section add—

"(8) In Scotland, "consumer contract" in this section has the same meaning as in section 12A(3) below."

(4) In section 15(1) after the definition of "hire purchase agreement" there is inserted—

""producer" means the manufacturer of goods, the importer of goods into the European Economic Area or any person purporting to be a producer by placing his name, trade mark or other distinctive sign on the goods;".

GENERAL NOTE

Regulation 13 amends section 10 of the Supply of Goods Act (Implied   **1–249**
Terms) Act 1973 in a way which is identical in all material respects to the amendments to section 14 of the Sale of Goods Act 1979 which are introduced by Regulation 3 and commented on above (see paras 1–062 *et seq.*). The relevant contracts are ones in which a creditor bails or hires goods under a hire-purchase agreement.

Amendments to the Unfair Contract Terms Act 1977

14.—(1) The Unfair Contract Terms Act 1977 is amended as follows.   **1–250**

(2) In section 12, after subsection (1) there is inserted the following subsection—

"(1A) But if the first party mentioned in subsection (1) is an individual paragraph (c) of that subsection must be ignored."

(3) For subsection (2) of section 12 there is substituted the following subsection—

"(2) But the buyer is not in any circumstances to be regarded as dealing as consumer—

 (a) if he is an individual and the goods are second hand goods sold at public auction at which individuals have the opportunity of attending the sale in person;

 (b) if he is not an individual and the goods are sold by auction or by competitive tender."

(4) In section 25—

 (a) in subsection (1), the definition of "consumer contract"—

  (i) after the word "means" there is inserted "subject to subsections (1A) and (1B) below";

  (ii) the words "(not being a contract of sale by auction or competitive tender)" are repealed.

 (b) after subsection (1) there is inserted—

"(1A) Where the consumer is an individual, paragraph (b) in the definition of "consumer contract" in subsection (1) must be disregarded.

(1B) The expression of "consumer contract" does not include a contract in which—

 (a) the buyer is an individual and the goods are second hand goods sold by public auction at which individuals have the opportunity of attending in person; or

 (b) the buyer is not an individual and the goods are sold by auction or competitive tender."

GENERAL NOTE

1–251 At first sight it may not be obvious why implementation of the Directive should have required an amendment to section 12 of the Unfair Contract Terms Act 1977 and thereby the definition of the expression "deals as consumer". The reason, as explained elsewhere (see above, para.1–001), is that although section 12 is concerned primarily with the scope of the ability to exclude or limit liability for breach of contract etc. (see generally *Benjamin*, paras 13–071—13–075) its definition has been adopted for the purposes of the Sale of Goods Act 1979 (see section 61(5A)) and the Directive has been implemented mainly by amendments to the 1979 Act. These various amendments to sections 14, 20, 32 and the new Part 5A remedies (see, respectively, Regulations 3 to 5) all apply where the buyer "deals as consumer". The same is true of the parallel amendments (see Regulations 7 to 11) to the Supply of Goods and Services Act 1982. In one respect the definition of "deals as consumer" in section 12 of the 1977 Act (and thus section 61(5A) of the 1979 Act) is more inclusive than the minimum harmonisation provisions of the Directive. As is noted below (see para.1–253; also above, para.1–024) a business and even a body corporate may on appropriate facts "deal as consumer". By way of contrast the Directive seeks to benefit only natural persons (individuals) who are acting for purposes which are not related to their trade, business or profession (see the definition of "consumer" in Article 1.2(a) and above, paras 1–054 *et seq.*). The more inclusive aspect of section 12, whereby there can be a corporate consumer, remains unchanged. But in two respects section 12 has required amendment to remove limitations which previously applied, though only as regards individuals. The first is that section 12(1)(c) with its requirement that the goods purchased be "of a type ordinarily supplied for private use or consumption" has no counterpart in the Directive where the definition of "consumer goods" (see Article 1.2(b)) is so wide as to place virtually no restrictions on the goods covered. Hence, by virtue of the new section 12(1A) section 12(1)(c) no longer applies where the buyer is "an individual" (as to which, see below, para.1–255). Secondly, the previous version of section 12(2) which excluded cases where the sale was by auction or by competitive tender did not meet the requirements of the Directive which permit only a more limited exclusion for the sale of second hand goods at certain public auctions (see Article 1.3). Hence section 12 has required further amendment in cases where the buyer is an individual in order to bring it into line with the Directive (see below, paras 1–256—1–257).

In its amended form section 12 of the Unfair Contract Terms Act 1977   **1–252**
now provides that:

(1) A party to a contract 'deals as consumer' in relation to another party if—

    (a) he neither makes the contract in the course of a business nor holds himself out as doing so; and

    (b) the other party does make the contract in the course of a business; and

    (c) in the case of a contract governed by the law of sale of goods or hire-purchase, or by section 7 of this Act, the goods passing under or in pursuance of the contract are of a type ordinarily supplied for private use or consumption.

(1A) But if the first party mentioned in subsection (1) is an individual paragraph (c) of that subsection must be ignored.

(2) But the buyer is not in any circumstances to be regarded as dealing as consumer—

    (a) if he is an individual and the goods are second hand goods sold at public auction at which individuals have the opportunity of attending the sale in person;

(b) if he is not an individual and the goods are sold by auction or by competitive tender.

(3) Subject to this, it is for those claiming that a party does not deal as consumer to show that he does not.

SECTION 12(1)(a) AND (b)

1–253   Section 12(1)(a) and (b) remain unchanged by the Regulations and are discussed in *Benjamin* (para.13–071). For present purposes it is sufficient to summarise their provisions. In the first place, it has been held that a business and even a company may deal as consumer provided that the purchase of the goods does not take place as an integral part of the business or as something which is necessarily incidental thereto (see *R&B Customs Brokers Ltd* v *United Dominions Trust Ltd* [1988] 1 W.L.R. 321; *Peter Symmons & Co* v *Cook* (1981) 131 N.L.J. 758). As was noted above (see para.1–251), this goes beyond the requirements of the Directive which benefits only natural persons who are acting for purposes which are not related to their trade, business or profession. Consequently, the extended protection could be revisited if this were thought appropriate. Secondly, the implications of the requirement of section 12(1)(b) that the other party, that is, the seller should make the contract "in the course of a business" are less clear. Two views are possible. One is that the same approach should be adopted as in section 12(1)(a) so that the sale would not be "in the course of a business" unless it formed an integral part of the business or was necessarily incidental to it. So, the one-off sale by a self-employed courier of his car (as in *Davies* v *Sumner* [1984] 1 W.L.R. 1301 where the context was criminal liability under the Trade Descriptions Act 1968), or by a farmer of his tractor or combined harvester, would not fall within section 12(1)(b) and the buyer would not deal as consumer. This would have the advantage of consistency of meaning within the same section. The alternative view is that section 12(1)(b) should be aligned, rather, with the approach taken when construing the words "in the course of a business" for the purposes of attracting the implied conditions of satisfactory quality and fitness for purpose of section 14 of the Sale of Goods Act 1979. In the context of section 14 such one-off transactions would be subject to the implied conditions, as was the sale by a fisherman of his working boat in *Stevenson* v *Rogers* [1999] Q.B. 1028 (see *Benjamin*, para.11–045). On balance, it is submitted that this latter interpretation is preferable as it extends the scope of protection accorded to consumers. On that basis, and assuming that any further requirements of section 12 are met (see below), the buyers in the transactions envisaged above would benefit from, for example, the new Part 5A remedies (see above, paras 1–095 *et seq.*), as well as from the protection against the operation of exemption and limitation clauses which the 1977 Act accords.

THE EFFECT OF SECTION 12(1A)

Section 12(1)(c) of the 1977 Act contains a further limitation to the   **1–254**
effect that a person will not deal as consumer unless the goods which he is buying are "of a type ordinarily supplied for private use or consumption". The scope of this expression is not without difficulty (see *Benjamin*, para.13–073) but, in any event, the new section 12(1A) requires that section 12(1)(c) be ignored when the buyer is "an individual".

THE MEANING OF "AN INDIVIDUAL"

The word "individual" is not defined in the Regulations or the 1977   **1–255**
Act. However, it seems substantially certain that it is to be interpreted as being synomous with the expression "natural person" which is the terminology adopted in the definition of a "consumer" in Article 1.2(a) of the Directive and in Regulation 2. Hence, as was noted above (see para. 1–055), an incorporated body would clearly not be an "individual". On the other hand, an unincorporated sole trader or an architect, solicitor, fisherman or farmer would be, as, of course, would be a person acting in a purely private capacity. The result might appear mildly surprising in that, assuming the requirements of section 12(1)(a) and (b) to be met, and those of section 12(2) (see below) not to come into play, all would then "deal as consumer" no matter what type of goods were being purchased. So, a successful solicitor or architect would appear to deal as consumer when buying a new jet aircraft in a one-off transaction for personal or business use, and would be entitled, for example, to invoke the new Part 5A remedies.

SALES BY AUCTION AND BY COMPETITIVE TENDER

Section 12(2) of the 1977 Act, as substituted by Regulation 14(3) of   **1–256**
the Regulations, excludes other transactions from the category of those in which buyers "deal as consumer". Again, a distinction is taken according to whether or not the buyer is an "individual" (as to which, see above, para. 1–255). A buyer other than an individual will not deal as consumer if the goods are sold by auction or competitive tender. This corresponds with the previous version of section 12(2) (see *Benjamin*, para.13–074). However, where the buyer is an

individual there is no equivalent provision for sales by competitive tender, and the exclusion of auction sales is limited to cases where "the goods are second hand goods sold at public auction at which individuals have the opportunity of attending the sale in person." This is permitted by Article 1.4 of the Directive which states that: "Member States may provide that the expression 'consumer goods' does not cover second-hand goods sold at public auction where consumers have the opportunity of attending the sale in person."

1–257 In a typical case of buying a second-hand car, furniture or a painting at a public auction the application of the new section 12(2)(a) will be straightforward. However, this may not always be so. For example, there may be difficulty in determining whether goods are second-hand. The word might be seen as synomous with "not previously owned" or the like and yet it seems clear that this is not so. Goods are typically sold from manufacturer to wholesaler to retailer, but they would not be described as "second-hand" simply by virtue of the fact that they had been sold on within the distribution chain. Nor is it clear that goods will invariably be second-hand once they have been sold *by* a consumer. For example, a private individual may buy fine wine, leaving it in storage in the merchant's cellars and later resell it to the merchant who, in turn, may resell at a public auction to a private buyer. It is unlikely that the last such sale is within section 12(2)(a) and hence one in which the final buyer does not enjoy the protected status of dealing as consumer. Probably, goods will be regarded as second-hand only if they have been used, or at least have been in the possession of someone who might be expected to use or consume them. This latter qualification seems necessary to cover situations in which unused and perhaps even unwrapped goods are sold off at auction (perhaps by an executor of an estate) in a house clearance sale.

The second requirement for the exclusion to apply is that the contract be made "at public auction at which individuals have the opportunity of attending the sale in person." Again this is not without difficulty. In order for the private buyer of second-hand goods not to be treated as dealing as consumer the auction must be "public" (as opposed, presumably, to one which is by invitation only) and there must be the opportunity of attending it in person. This would not be the case where it is held exclusively over the internet or by telephone or postal bidding. However, where a public auction of second-hand goods may be attended in person, an individual will not deal as consumer simply because he has chosen to avail himself of an alternative option of putting in a telephone or postal bid. The question is whether individuals had the opportunity of attending in person, not whether they availed themselves of such an opportunity.

THE ONUS OF PROOF

Section 12(3) provides that, subject to the provisions of section 12(1)   **1–258**
and (2), "it is for those claiming that a party does not deal as consumer
to show that he does not." This is re-enforced by the definition in section 61(5A) of the Sale of Goods Act 1979 which provides in part that
"it is for a seller claiming that the buyer does not deal as consumer to
show that he does not."

RELATED ISSUES

The question of excluding or limiting liability under the Unfair Con-   **1–259**
tract Terms Act 1977 and the Unfair Terms in Consumer Contracts
Regulations 1999 is also discussed above in the context of the amendments to sections 20 and 32 of the Sale of Goods Act (passing of risk
and acceptance of goods in consumer cases) (see para. 1–093) and the
new Part 5A remedies (see paras 1–219—1–221).

Consumer guarantees

15.—(1) Where goods are sold or otherwise supplied to a consumer   **1–260**
which are offered with a consumer guarantee, the consumer guarantee
takes effect at the time the goods are delivered as a contractual obligation
owed by the guarantor under the conditions set out in the guarantee statement and the associated advertising.

(2) The guarantor shall ensure that the guarantee sets out in plain intelligible language the contents of the guarantee and the essential particulars
necessary for making claims under the guarantee, notably the duration
and territorial scope of the guarantee as well as the name and address of
the guarantor.

(3) On request by the consumer to a person to whom paragraph (4)
applies, the guarantee shall within a reasonable time be made available in
writing or in another durable medium available and accessible to him.

(4) This paragraph applies to the guarantor and any other person who
offers to consumers the goods which are the subject of the guarantee for
sale or supply.

(5) Where consumer goods are offered with a consumer guarantee, and
where those goods are offered within the territory of the United Kingdom,
then the guarantor shall ensure that the consumer guarantee is written in
English.

(6) If the guarantor fails to comply with the provisions of paragraphs (2)
or (5) above, or a person to whom paragraph (4) applies fails to comply
with paragraph (3) then the enforcement authority may apply for an
injunction or (in Scotland) an order of specific implement against that person requiring him to comply.

(7) The court on application under this Regulation may grant an injunction or (in Scotland) an order of specific implement on such terms as it
thinks fit.

GENERAL NOTE

1–261   Regulation 15 is a free-standing provision in the sense that it does not operate by way of amendment to the Sale of Goods Act or other legislation. Relevant definitions of key words (notably, "goods", "supplied", "consumer", "consumer guarantee", "guarantor", "enforcement authority" and "court") are contained in Regulation 2 (see above, paras 1–052—1–061). In particular, it should be noted that the reference is to a "consumer" which is a more restrictive expression than a person who "deals as consumer" (see above, paras 1–024—1–026 and 1–251). Regulation 15 corresponds to Article 6 of Directive 1999/44/EC, the latter being discussed in *Benjamin*, paras 14–067—14–069. Neither the Regulations nor the Directive impose any obligation to provide a consumer guarantee, nor require that any such guarantee should have a minimum substantive content. The purpose, rather, is to make an undertaking which has been given voluntarily legally binding on the guarantor, subject to the conditions contained therein and in any associated advertising. This should remove the need for determining whether, on a traditional analysis, a contract has been concluded between a manufacturer of goods and the consumer. Hence it will not be necessary to inquire whether an offer of a guarantee (for example, of electrical equipment) has been accepted or consideration given (for example, by completing and posting a registration slip) in exchange for the undertaking contained in it. Regulation 15(1) provides that the guarantee takes effect as a contractual obligation without more.

REGULATION 15(1)

1–262   The operation of this provision should be relatively straightforward where the consumer who is claiming on the guarantee is the original purchaser or transferee of the goods. Following the wording of Regulation 15(1), the goods will have been "sold or otherwise supplied" to him and the guarantee will take effect according to its terms. The position where the person claiming on the guarantee is a donee or even a sub-purchaser from the original consumer is less clear since Regulation 15(1) and Article 6 are silent as to the question of to whom the contractual obligation is owed. Also, no clarification is afforded by the definition of a "consumer guarantee" in Regulation 2 (see above, para. 1–058) since this simply refers to "any undertaking to a consumer". A number of scenarios might be envisaged. For example, the guarantee may be expressed as being non-transferable. In that case it will benefit the original purchaser or transferee only. Conversely, it may state that it is fully transferable or the like—in which case the donee, etc. should benefit from it since the relevant provisions do not in terms require that the goods should have been sold or otherwise supplied (within the meaning of Regulation 2) to him. The intermediate case is that where the guarantee makes no reference to the issue of transferability. On balance, it is submitted that it should be impliedly understood as benefiting any recipient who is a "consumer" (that is, a natural person acting for purposes which are outside his trade, business or profession: see Regulation 2, above, paras 1–054—1–057), provided, at least, that the original purchaser or transferee was also a consumer. Some slender support for this view might be derived from a change in wording between the draft Regulations, which referred to the contractual obligation being "owed to the consumer" (which might be thought to refer back to the original consumer), and the final version, where these words are omitted.

REGULATION 15(2)

Regulation 15(2) corresponds to part of Article 6.2 of the Directive, **1–263** (the second indent), the reference to "plain intelligible language" echoing that of Regulation 7(1) of the Unfair Terms in Consumer Contracts Regulations 1999 (SI 1999/2083).

REGULATION 15(3) AND (4)

Regulation 15(3) and (4) corresponds to Article 6.3 of the Directive. **1–264** There are potential problems of interpretation with several of the main elements of the requirement. First, satisfying the obligation to make the guarantee available within a "reasonable time" on request by the consumer will presumably depend in part on whether one is concerned with the "guarantor" or with some other person (for example, a retailer) who is within the scope of Regulation 15(4). Generally, it may be assumed, the guarantor will be in the better position to do this relatively speedily. Secondly, the reference in Regulation 15(4) to a person who "offers to consumers the goods which are the subject of the guarantee for sale or supply" is clearly not to be understood in a technical sense. In the standard transaction it would usually be the consumer buyer who makes the offer, not the retail seller, although the latter would accept it (see, for example, *Fisher* v *Bell* [1961] 1 Q.B. 394 and *Pharmaceutical Society of Great Britain* v *Boots Cash Chemists (Southern) Ltd* [1952] 2 Q.B. 795; *Benjamin*, para.2–002). However, for the purposes of Regulation 15(4) it is plainly the retailer who is to be treated as making the offer of the goods for sale etc. so as to be subject to the obligations of Regulation 15(3). Finally, there are doubts about how the guarantor or other relevant person might satisfy the requirement of Regulation 15(3) of making the guarantee available to the consumer "in writing or in another durable medium available and accessible to him". The same form of words is used in, for example, Regulation 8(1) of the Consumer Protection (Distance Selling) Regulations 2000 (SI 2000/2334) and it is commented on in *Benjamin*, para.14–052.

REGULATION 15(5)

1–265   Where goods are "offered [see the note to Regulation 15(3) and (4), above] within the territory of the United Kingdom" the guarantor must ensure that the consumer guarantee is written in English. This is permitted by Article 6.4 of the Directive. One curiosity about this provision is that it is linked (unlike the rest of Regulation 15) to "consumer goods". The term is not defined in the Regulations, but no doubt it should be interpreted in line with Article 1.2(b) of the Directive so as to mean "any tangible movable item, with the exception of:—goods sold by way of execution or otherwise by authority of law,—water and gas where they are not put up for sale in a limited volume or set quantity,—electricity". Obviously this is a very broad definition and is unlikely to limit the scope of Regulation 15(5).

REGULATION 15(6) AND (7)

1–266   Although the point is not spelt out expressly in Regulation 15, it is clear that non-compliance with Regulation 15(2), (3) and (5) will not affect the binding nature of the guarantee. Indeed, Article 6.5 of the Directive states that: "Should a guarantee infringe the requirements of paragraphs 2, 3 or 4 [of Article 6], the validly of this guarantee shall in no way be affected, and the consumer can still rely on the guarantee and require that it be honoured."

1–267   The method of ensuring compliance with the obligations imposed by the above provisions is for the relevant enforcement authority to apply for an injunction which, if granted and broken, might ultimately lead to a potential fine or imprisonment for contempt of court. The definition of an "enforcement authority" in Regulation 2 (see above, paras 1–052, 1–059) is relatively tightly confined and, the Stop Now Orders (EC Directive) Regulations 2001 (SI2001/1422) provided an alternative method of control (see reg.2(3)(j) and Sch.1 and the discussion in *Benjamin*, paras 14–121—14–124). These Regulations have been revoked and replaced with effect from June 20, 2003 by the enforcement provisions of Part 8 of the Enterprise Act 2002: see the Enterprise Act 2002 (Commencement No. 3, Transitional and Transitory Provisions and Savings Order 2003) (SI 2003/1397). Directive 1999/44/EC is a "listed Directive" for the purposes of the Community infringement provisions of Part 8 (and see also Sch.13) which implements Directive 98/27/EC of the European Parliament and of the Council (the Injunctions Directive"). Also, Regulation 15 of the Sale and Supply of Goods to Consumers Regulations 2002 is listed as a corresponding specified UK law giving effect to part of Directive 1999/44/EC: see the Enterprise Act 2002 (Part 8 Community Infringements Specified UK Laws) Order 2003 (SI 2003/1374) Article 3 and Schedule.

Although the Regulations do not make any reference to the point, it is **1–268** clear in principle that the granting of an injunction is not the sole remedy potentially available. The consumer guarantee takes effect "as a contractual obligation owed by the guarantor" and situations may occur in which a claimant suffers loss by virtue of non-compliance with the obligations imposed by Regulation 15(2), (3) or (5). For example, he may be unable to benefit from the guarantee because it was not made available to him in writing (or in another sufficient form) and within a reasonable time or it was not written in English. In such circumstances an action for damages for breach of contract should be available against the guarantor. It is less clear that a similar contractual claim would lie against a person (other than a guarantor) who is subject to Regulation 15(3) by virtue of being within the scope of Regulation 15(4). Such a person is not a "guarantor" who owes the contractual obligation for the purposes of Regulation 15(1).

A FURTHER PROVISION

Article 6.2, provides in part (see the first indent) that: "The guarantee **1–269** shall:—state that the consumer has legal rights under applicable national legislation governing the sale of consumer goods and make clear that those rights are not affected by the guarantee." This provision does not have a counterpart in the Sale and Supply of Goods to Consumers Regulations. However, Article 5 of the Consumer Transactions (Restrictions on Statements) Order 1976 (SI 1976/1813, as amended by SI 1978/127), covers broadly the same ground. In general terms this seeks to prevent consumers from being misled into believing that such guarantees represent the totality of their legal rights in the event of goods proving to be defective. However, two points should be noted. First, breach of Article 5 is potentially a criminal offence under section 23 of the Fair Trading Act 1973 and not simply a basis for seeking an injunction. Secondly, the Order does not in terms require the guarantor to state that "the consumer has legal rights". The requirement is, rather, to state that the guarantee "does not or will not affect the statutory rights of a consumer." The existence of such rights is thus left to be implied, rather than stated or still less described. Finally, it should be noted that section 5 of the Unfair Contract Terms Act 1977 controls attempts to exclude or restrict liability through a document purporting to be a "guarantee". Section 5(1) provides that: "in the case of goods of a type ordinarily supplied for private use or consumption, where loss or damage—(a) arises from the goods proving defective while in consumer use; and (b) results from the negligence of a person concerned in the manufacture or distribution of the goods, liability for the loss or damage cannot be excluded or restricted by reference to any contract term or notice contained in or operating by reference to a guarantee of the goods". Section 5 does not apply as between the parties to a contract under or in pursuance of which possession or ownership of the goods passed. Such contract are subject to control, rather, under sections 6(2) and 7(2) of the 1977 Act. For a discussion of section 5, see *Benjamin*, para. 14–066.

APPENDIX A

Amendments up to and including those introduced by the Sale and Supply of Goods to Consumers Regulations 2002 are indicated by bold side lines.

Sale of Goods Act 1979

(1979 c.54)

An Act to consolidate the law relating to the sale of goods. [6th December, 1979]   **A–001**

PART I

CONTRACTS TO WHICH ACT APPLIES

Contracts to which Act applies

1.—(1) This Act applies to contracts of sale of goods made on or after (but not to those made before) 1 January 1894.

(2) In relation to contracts made on certain dates, this Act applies subject to the modification of certain of its sections as mentioned in Schedule 1 below.

(3) Any such modification is indicated in the section concerned by a reference to Schedule 1 below.

(4) Accordingly, where a section does not contain such a reference, this Act applies in relation to the contract concerned without such modification of the section.

PART II

FORMATION OF THE CONTRACT

Contract of Sale

Contract of sale

2.—(1) A contract of sale of goods is a contract by which the seller transfers or agrees to transfer the property in goods to the buyer for a money consideration, called the price.

(2) There may be a contract of sale between one part owner and another.

(3) A contract of sale may be absolute or conditional.

(4) Where under a contract of sale the property in the goods is transferred from the seller to the buyer the contract is called a sale.

(5) Where under a contract of sale the transfer of the property in the goods is to take place at a future time or subject to some condition later to be fulfilled the contract is called an agreement to sell.

(6) An agreement to sell becomes a sale when the time elapses or the conditions are fulfilled subject to which the property in the goods is to be transferred.

Capacity to buy and sell

3.—(1) Capacity to buy and sell is regulated by the general law concerning capacity to contract and to transfer and acquire property.

(2) Where necessaries are sold and delivered to a minor or to a person who by reason of mental incapacity or drunkenness is incompetent to contract, he must pay a reasonable price for them.

(3) In subsection (2) above "necessaries" means goods suitable to the condition in life of the minor or other person concerned and to his actual requirements at the time of the sale and delivery.

Formalities of Contract

How contract of sale is made

4.—(1) Subject to this and any other Act, a contract of sale may be made in writing (either with or without seal), or by word of mouth, or partly in writing and partly by word of mouth, or may be implied from the conduct of the parties.

(2) Nothing in this section affects the law relating to corporations.

Subject-Matter of Contract

Existing or future goods

5.—(1) The goods which form the subject of a contract of sale may be either existing goods, owned or possessed by the seller, or goods to be manufactured or acquired by him after the making of the contract of sale, in this Act called future goods.

(2) There may be a contract for the sale of goods the acquisition of which by the seller depends on a contingency which may or may not happen.

(3) Whereby a contract of sale the seller purports to effect a present sale of future goods, the contract operates as an agreement to sell the goods.

Goods which have perished

6.—Where there is a contract for the sale of specific goods, and the goods without the knowledge of the seller have perished at the time when the contract is made, the contract is void.

Goods perishing before the sale but after agreement to sell

7.—Where there is an agreement to sell specific goods and subsequently the goods, without any fault on the part of the seller or buyer, perish before the risk passes to the buyer, the agreement is avoided.

The Price

Ascertainment of price

8.—(1) The price in a contract of sale may be fixed by the contract, or may be left to be fixed in a manner agreed by the contract, or may be determined by the course of dealing between the parties.

(2) Where the price is not determined as mentioned in subsection (1) above the buyer must pay a reasonable price.

(3) What is a reasonable price is a question of fact dependent on the circumstances of each particular case.

Agreement to sell at valuation

9.—(1) Where there is an agreement to sell goods on the terms that the price is to be fixed by the valuation of a third party, and he cannot or does not make the valuation, the agreement is avoided; but if the goods or any part of them have been delivered to and appropriated by the buyer he must pay a reasonable price for them.

(2) Where the third party is prevented from making the valuation by the fault of the seller or buyer, the party not at fault may maintain an action for damages against the party at fault.

Implied terms etc.   I

Stipulations about time

10.—(1) Unless a different intention appears from the terms of the contract, stipulations as to time of payment are not of the essence of a contract of sale.

(2) Whether any other stipulation as to time is or is not of the essence of the contract depends on the terms of the contract.

(3) In a contract of sale "month" prima facie means calendar month.

When condition to be treated as warranty

11.—(1) This section does not apply to Scotland.

(2) Where a contract of sale is subject to a condition to be fulfilled by the seller, the buyer may waive the condition, or may elect to treat the breach of the condition as a breach of warranty and not as a ground for treating the contract as repudiated.

(3) Whether a stipulation in a contract of sale is a condition, the breach of which may give rise to a right to treat the contract as repudiated, or a warranty, the breach of which may give rise to a claim for damages but not to a right to reject the goods and treat the contract as repudiated, depends in each case on the construction of the contract; and a stipulation may be a condition, though called a warranty in the contract.

(4) Subject to s.35A below, where a contract of sale is not severable and the buyer has accepted the goods or part of them, the breach of a condition to be fulfilled by the seller can only be treated as a breach of warranty, and not as a ground for rejecting the goods and treating the contract as repudiated, unless there is an express or implied term of the contract to that effect.

(5) [*Repealed.*]

(6) Nothing in this section affects a condition or warranty whose fulfilment is excused by law by reason of impossibility or otherwise.

(7) Paragraph 2 of Schedule 1 below applies in relation to a contract made before 22 April 1967 or (in the application of this Act to Northern Ireland) 28 July 1967.

Implied terms about title, etc.

12.—(1) In a contract of sale, other than one to which subsection (3) below applies, there is an implied term on the part of the seller that in the case of a sale he has a right to sell the goods, and in the case of an agreement to sell he will have such a right at the time when the property is to pass.

(2) In a contract of sale, other than one to which subsection (3) below applies, there is also an implied term that—

(a) the goods are free, and will remain free until the time when the property is to pass, from any charge or encumbrance not disclosed or known to the buyer before the contract is made, and

(b) the buyer will enjoy quiet possession of the goods except so far as it may be disturbed by the owner or other person entitled to the benefit of any charge or encumbrance so disclosed or known.

(3) This subsection applies to a contract of sale in the case of which there appears from the contract or is to be inferred from its circumstances an inten-

tion that the seller should transfer only such title as he or a third person may have.

(4) In a contract to which subsection (3) above applies there is an implied term that all charges or encumbrances known to the seller and not known to the buyer have been disclosed to the buyer before the contract is made.

(5) In a contract to which subsection (3) above applies there is also an implied term that none of the following will disturb the buyer's quiet possession of the goods, namely—

(a) the seller;

(b) in a case where the parties to the contract intend that the seller should transfer only such title as a third person may have, that person;

(c) anyone claiming through or under the seller or that third person otherwise than under a charge or encumbrance disclosed or known to the buyer before the contract is made.

(5A) As regards England and Wales and Northern Ireland, the term implied by subsection (1) above is a condition and the terms implied by subsections (2), (4) and (5) above are warranties.

(6) Paragraph 3 of Schedule 1 below applies in relation to a contract made before 18 May 1973.

Sale by description

13.—(1) Where there is a contract for the sale of goods by description, there is an implied term that the goods will correspond with the description.

(1A) As regards England and Wales and Northern Ireland, the term implied by subsection (1) above is a condition.

(2) If the sale is by sample as well as by description it is not sufficient that the bulk of the goods corresponds with the sample if the goods do not also correspond with the description.

(3) A sale of goods is not prevented from being a sale by description by reason only that, being exposed for sale or hire, they are selected by the buyer.

(4) Paragraph 4 of Schedule 1 below applies in relation to a contract made before 18 May 1973.

Implied terms about quality or fitness

14.—(1) Except as provided by this section and section 15 below and subject to any other enactment, there is no implied term about the quality or fitness for any particular purpose of goods supplied under a contract of sale.

(2) Where the seller sells goods in the course of a business, there is an implied term that the goods supplied under the contract are of satisfactory quality.

(2A) For the purposes of this Act, goods are of satisfactory quality if they meet the standard that a reasonable person would regard as satisfactory, taking account of any description of the goods, the price (if relevant) and all the other relevant circumstances.

(2B) For the purposes of this Act, the quality of goods includes their state and condition and the following (among others) are in appropriate cases aspects of the quality of goods—

(a) fitness for all the purposes for which goods of the kind in question are commonly supplied,

(b) appearance and finish,

(c) freedom from minor defects,

(d) safety, and

(e) durability.

(2C) The term implied by subsection (2) above does not extend to any matter making the quality of goods unsatisfactory—

(a) which is specifically drawn to the buyer's attention before the contract is made,

(b) where the buyer examines the goods before the contract is made, which that examination ought to reveal, or

(c) in the case of a contract for sale by sample, which would have been apparent on a reasonable examination of the sample.

(2D) If the buyer deals as consumer or, in Scotland, if a contract of sale is a consumer contract, the relevant circumstances mentioned in subsection (2A) above include any public statements on the specific characteristics of the goods mde about them by the seller, the producer or his representative, particularly in advertising or on labelling.

(2E) A public statement is not by virtue of subsection (2D) above a relevant circumstance for the purposes of subsection (2A) above in the case of a contract of sale, if the seller shows that—

(a) at the time the contract was made, he was not, and could not reasonably have been, aware of the statement,

(b) before the contract was made, the statement had been withdrawn in public or, to the extent that it contained anything which was incorrect or misleading, it had been corrected in public, or

(c) the decision to buy the goods could not have been influenced by the statement.

(2F) Subsections (2D) and (2E) above do not prevent any public statement from being a relevant circumstance for the purposes of subsection (2A) above (whether or not the buyer deals as consumer or, in Scotland, whether or not the contract of sale is a consumer contract) if the statement would have been such a circumstance apart from those subsections.

(3) Where the seller sells goods in the course of a business and the buyer, expressly or by implication, makes known—

    (a) to the seller, or

    (b) where the purchase price or part of it is payable by instalments and the goods were previously sold by a credit-broker to the seller, to that credit-broker,

for any particular purpose for which the goods are being bought, there is an implied term that the goods supplied under the contract are reasonably fit for that purpose, whether or not that is a purpose for which such goods are commonly supplied, except where the circumstances show that the buyer does not rely, or that it is unreasonable for him to rely, on the skill or judgment of the seller or credit-broker.

(4) An implied term about quality or fitness for a particular purpose may be annexed to a contract of sale by usage.

(5) The preceding provisions of this section apply to a sale by a person who in the course of a business is acting as agent for another as they apply to a sale by a principal in the course of a business, except where that other is not selling in the course of a business and either the buyer knows that fact or reasonable steps are taken to bring it to the notice of the buyer before the contract is made.

(6) As regards England and Wales and Northern Ireland, the terms implied by subsections (2) and (3) above are conditions.

(7) Paragraph 5 of Schedule 1 below applies in relation to a contract made on or after 18 May 1973 and before the appointed day, and paragraph 6 in relation to one made before 18 May 1973.

(8) In subsection (7) above and paragraph 5 of Schedule 1 below references to the appointed day are to the day appointed for the purposes of those provisions by an order of the Secretary of State made by statutory instrument.

Sale by Sample

Sale by sample

    15.—(1) A contract of sale is a contract for sale by sample where there is an express or implied term to that effect in the contract.

    (2) In the case of a contract for sale by sample there is an implied term—

(a) that the bulk will correspond with the sample in quality;

(b) [*Repealed*];

(c) that the goods will be free from any defect, making their quality unsatisfactory, which would not be apparent on reasonable examination of the sample.

(3) As regards England and Wales and Northern Ireland, the term implied by subsection (2) above is a condition.

(4) Paragraph 7 of Schedule 1 below applies in relation to a contract made before 18 May 1973.

Modification of remedies for breach of condition in non-consumer cases

15A.—(1) Where in the case of a contract of sale—

(a) the buyer would, apart from this subsection, have the right to reject goods by reason of a breach on the part of the seller of a term implied by section 13, 14 or 15 above, but

(b) the breach is so slight that it would be unreasonable for him to reject them,

then, if the buyer does not deal as consumer, the breach is not to be treated as a breach of condition but may be treated as a breach of warranty.

(2) This section applies unless a contrary intention appears in, or is to be implied from, the contract.

(3) It is for the seller to show that a breach fell within subsection (1)(b) above.

(4) This section does not apply to Scotland.

Remedies for breach of contract as respects Scotland

15B.—(1) Where in a contract of sale the seller is in breach of any term of the contract (express or implied), the buyer shall be entitled—

(a) to claim damages, and

(b) if the breach is material, to reject any goods delivered under the contract and treat it as repudiated.

(2) Where a contract of sale is a consumer contract, then, for the purposes of subsection (1)(b) above, breach by the seller of any term (express or implied)—

(a) as to the quality of the goods or their fitness for a purpose,

(b) if the goods are, or are to be, sold by description, that the goods will correspond with the description,

(c) if the goods are, or are to be, sold by reference to a sample, that the bulk will correspond with the sample in quality,

shall be deemed to be a material breach.

(3) This section applies to Scotland only.

PART III

EFFECTS OF THE CONTRACT

Transfer of Property as between Seller and Buyer

Goods must be ascertained

16. Subject to section 20A below where there is a contract for the sale of unascertained goods no property in the goods is transferred to the buyer unless and until the goods are ascertained.

Property passes when intended to pass

17.—(1) Where there is a contract for the sale of specific or ascertained goods the property in them is transferred to the buyer at such time as the parties to the contract intend it to be transferred.

(2) For the purpose of ascertaining the intention of the parties regard shall be had to the terms of the contract, the conduct of the parties and the circumstances of the case.

Rules for ascertaining intention

18. Unless a different intention appears, the following are rules for ascertaining the intention of the parties as to the time at which the property in the goods is to pass to the buyer.

Rule 1.—Where there is an unconditional contract for the sale of specific goods in a deliverable state the property in the goods passes to the buyer when the contract is made, and it is immaterial whether the time of payment or the time of delivery, or both, be postponed.

Rule 2.—Where there is a contract for the sale of specific goods and the seller is bound to do something to the goods for the purpose of putting them into a deliverable state, the property does not pass until the thing is done and the buyer has notice that it has been done.

Rule 3.—Where there is a contract for the sale of specific goods in a deliverable state but the seller is bound to weigh, measure, test, or do some other act or thing with reference to the goods for the purpose of ascertaining the price, the property does not pass until the act or thing is done and the buyer has notice that it has been done.

Rule 4.—When goods are delivered to the buyer on approval or on sale or return or other similar terms the property in the goods passes to the buyer:—

(a) when he signifies his approval or acceptance to the seller or does any other act adopting the transaction;

(b) if he does not signify his approval or acceptance to the seller but retains the goods without giving notice of rejection, then, if a time has been fixed for the return of the goods, on the expiration of that time, and, if no time has been fixed, on the expiration of a reasonable time.

Rule 5.—(1) Where there is a contract for the sale of unascertained or future goods by description, and goods of that description and in a deliverable state are unconditionally appropriated to the contract, either by the seller with the assent of the buyer or by the buyer with the assent of the seller, the property in the goods then passes to the buyer; and the assent may be express or implied, and may be given either before or after the appropriation is made.

(2) Where, in pursuance of the contract, the seller delivers the goods to the buyer or to a carrier or other bailee or custodier (whether named by the buyer or not) for the purpose of transmission to the buyer, and does not reserve the right of disposal, he is to be taken to have unconditionally appropriated the goods to the contract.

(3) Where there is a contract for the sale of a specified quantity of unascertained goods in a deliverable state forming part of a bulk which is identified either in the contract or by subsequent agreement between the parties and the bulk is reduced to (or to less than) that quantity, then if the buyer under that contract is the only buyer to whom goods are then due out of the bulk—

(a) the remaining goods are to be taken as appropriated to that contract at the time when the bulk is so reduced; and

(b) the property in those goods then passes to that buyer.

(4) Paragraph (3) above applies also (with the necessary modifications) where a bulk is reduced to (or to less than) the aggregate of the quantities due to a single buyer under separate contracts relating to that bulk and he is the only buyer to whom goods are then due out of that bulk.

Reservation of right of disposal

19.—(1) Where there is a contract for the sale of specific goods or where goods are subsequently appropriated to the contract, the seller may, by the terms of the contract or appropriation, reserve the right of disposal of the goods until certain conditions are fulfilled; and in such a case, notwithstanding the delivery of the goods to the buyer, or to a carrier or other bailee or custodier for the purpose of transmission to the buyer, the property in the goods does not pass to the buyer until the conditions imposed by the seller are fulfilled.

(2) Where goods are shipped, and by the bill of lading the goods are deliverable to the order of the seller or his agent, the seller is prima facie to be taken to reserve the right of disposal.

(3) Where the seller of goods draws on the buyer for the price, and transmits the bill of exchange and bill of lading to the buyer together to secure acceptance or payment of the bill of exchange, the buyer is bound to return the bill of lading if he does not honour the bill of exchange, and if he wrongfully retains the bill of lading the property in the goods does not pass to him.

Passing of risk

20.—(1) Unless otherwise agreed, the goods remain at the seller's risk until the property in them is transferred to the buyer, but when the property in them is transferred to the buyer the goods are at the buyer's risk whether delivery has been made or not.

(2) But where delivery has been delayed through the fault of either buyer or seller the goods are at the risk of the party at fault as regards any loss which might not have occurred but for such fault.

(3) Nothing in this section affects the duties or liabilities of either seller or buyer as a bailee or custodier of the goods of the other party.

(4) In a case where the buyer deals as consumer or, in Scotland, where there is a consumer contract in which the buyer is a consumer, subsections (1) to (3) above must be ignored and the goods remain at the seller's risk until they are delivered to the consumer.

Undivided shares in goods forming part of a bulk

20A.—(1) This section applies to a contract for the sale of a specified quantity of unascertained goods if the following conditions are met—

(a) the goods or some of them form part of a bulk which is identified either in the contract or by subsequent agreement between the parties; and

(b) the buyer has paid the price for some or all of the goods which are the subject of the contract and which form part of the bulk.

(2) Where this section applies, then (unless the parties agree otherwise), as soon as the conditions specified in paragraphs (a) and (b) of subsection (1) above are met or at such later time as the parties may agree—

(a) property in an undivided share in the bulk is transferred to the buyer, and

(b) the buyer becomes an owner in common of the bulk.

(3) Subject to subsection (4) below, for the purposes of this section, the undivided share of a buyer in a bulk at any time shall be such share as the quantity of goods paid for and due to the buyer out of the bulk bears to the quantity of goods in the bulk at that time.

(4) Where the aggregate of the undivided shares of buyers in a bulk determined under subsection (3) above would at any time exceed the whole of the bulk at that time, the undivided share in the bulk of each buyer shall be reduced proportionately so that the aggregate of the undivided shares is equal to the whole bulk.

(5) Where a buyer has paid the price for only some of the goods due to him out of a bulk, any delivery to the buyer out of the bulk shall, for the purposes of this section, be ascribed in the first place to the goods in respect of which payment has been made.

(6) For the purposes of this section payment of part of the price for any goods shall be treated as payment for a corresponding part of the goods.

Deemed consent by co-owner to dealings in bulk goods

20B.—(1) A person who has become an owner in common of a bulk by virtue of section 20A above shall be deemed to have consented to—

(a) any delivery of goods out of the bulk to any other owner in common of the bulk, being goods which are due to him under his contract;

(b) any dealing with or removal, delivery or disposal of goods in the bulk by any other person who is an owner in common of the bulk in so far as the goods fall within that co-owner's undivided share in the bulk at the time of the dealing, removal, delivery or disposal.

(2) No cause of action shall accrue to anyone against a person by reason of that person having acted in accordance with paragraph (a) or (b) of subsection (1) above in reliance on any consent deemed to have been given under that subsection.

(3) Nothing in this section or section 20A above shall—

(a) impose an obligation on a buyer of goods out of a bulk to compensate any other buyer of goods out of that bulk for any shortfall in the goods received by that other buyer;

(b) affect any contractual arrangement between buyers of goods out of a bulk for adjustments between themselves; or

(c) affect the rights of any buyer under his contract.

Transfer of Title

Sale by person not the owner

21.—(1) Subject to this Act, where goods are sold by a person who is not their owner, and who does not sell them under the authority or with the consent of the owner, the buyer acquires no better title to the goods than the seller had, unless the owner of the goods is by his conduct precluded from denying the seller's authority to sell.

(2) Nothing in this Act affects—

  (a) the provisions of the Factors Acts or any enactment enabling the apparent owner of goods to dispose of them as if he were their true owner;

  (b) the validity of any contract of sale under any special common law or statutory power of sale or under the order of a court of competent jurisdiction.

Market overt

22.—(1) [*Repealed.*]

(2) This section does not apply to Scotland.

(3) Paragraph 8 of Schedule 1 below applies in relation to a contract under which goods were sold before 1 January 1968 or (in the application of this Act to Northern Ireland) 29 August 1967.

Sale under voidable title

23. When the seller of goods has a voidable title to them, but his title has not been avoided at the time of the sale, the buyer acquires a good title to the goods, provided he buys them in good faith and without notice of the seller's defect of title.

Seller in possession after sale

24. Where a person having sold goods continues or is in possession of the goods, or of the documents of title to the goods, the delivery or transfer by that person, or by a mercantile agent acting for him, of the goods or documents of title under any sale, pledge, or other disposition thereof, to any person receiving the same in good faith and without notice of the previous sale, has the same effect as if the person making the delivery or transfer were expressly authorised by the owner of the goods to make the same.

Buyer in possession after sale

25.—(1) Where a person having bought or agreed to buy goods obtains, with the consent of the seller, possession of the goods or the documents of title to the goods, the delivery or transfer by that person, or by a mercantile agent acting for him, of the goods or documents of title, under any sale, pledge, or other disposition thereof, to any person receiving the same in good faith and without notice of any lien or other right of the original seller in respect of the goods, has the same effect as if the person making the delivery or transfer were a mercantile agent in possession of the goods or documents of title with the consent of the owner.

(2) For the purposes of subsection (1) above—

(a) the buyer under a conditional sale agreement is to be taken not to be a person who has bought or agreed to buy goods, and

(b) "conditional sale agreement" means an agreement for the sale of goods which is a consumer credit agreement within the meaning of the Consumer Credit Act 1974 under which the purchase price or part of it is payable by instalments, and the property in the goods is to remain in the seller (notwithstanding that the buyer is to be in possession of the goods) until such conditions as to the payment of instalments or otherwise as may be specified in the agreement are fulfilled.

(3) Paragraph 9 of Schedule 1 below applies in relation to a contract under which a person buys or agrees to buy goods and which is made before the appointed day.*

(4) In subsection (3) above and paragraph 9 of Schedule 1 below references to the appointed day are to the day appointed for the purposes of those provisions by an order of the Secretary of State made by statutory instrument.

Supplementary to sections 24 and 25

26. In sections 24 and 25 above "mercantile agent" means a mercantile agent having in the customary course of his business as such agent authority either—

(a) to sell goods, or

(b) to consign goods for the purpose of sale, or

(c) to buy goods, or

(d) to raise money on the security of goods.

---

*(SI 1983/1572) appointed May 19, 1985, for the purposes of subs.(3).

PART VI

PERFORMANCE OF THE CONTRACT

Duties of seller and buyer

27. It is the duty of the seller to deliver the goods, and of the buyer to accept and pay for them, in accordance with the terms of the contract of sale.

Payment and delivery are concurrent conditions

28. Unless otherwise agreed, delivery of the goods and payment of the price are concurrent conditions, that is to say, the seller must be ready and willing to give possession of the goods to the buyer in exchange for the price and the buyer must be ready and willing to pay the price in exchange for possession of the goods.

Rules about delivery

29.—(1) Whether it is for the buyer to take possession of the goods or for the seller to send them to the buyer is a question depending in each case on the contract, express or implied, between the parties.

(2) Apart from any such contract, express or implied, the place of delivery is the seller's place of business if he has one, and if not, his residence; except that, if the contract is for the sale of specific goods, which to the knowledge of the parties when the contract is made are in some other place, then that place is the place of delivery.

(3) Where under the contract of sale the seller is bound to send the goods to the buyer, but no time for sending them is fixed, the seller is bound to send them within a reasonable time.

(4) Where the goods at the time of sale are in the possession of a third person, there is no delivery by seller to buyer unless and until the third person acknowledges to the buyer that he holds the goods on his behalf; but nothing in this section affects the operation of the issue or transfer of any document of title to goods.

(5) Demand or tender of delivery may be treated as ineffectual unless made at a reasonable hour; and what is a reasonable hour is a question of fact.

(6) Unless otherwise agreed, the expenses of and incidental to putting the goods into a deliverable state must be borne by the seller.

Delivery of wrong quantity

30.—(1) Where the seller delivers to the buyer a quantity of goods less than he contracted to sell, the buyer may reject them, but if the buyer accepts the goods so delivered he must pay for them at the contract rate.

(2) Where the seller delivers to the buyer a quantity of goods larger than he contracted to sell, the buyer may accept the goods included in the contract and reject the rest, or he may reject the whole.

(2A) A buyer who does not deal as consumer may not—

(a) where the seller delivers a quantity of goods less than he contracted to sell, reject the goods under subsection (1) above, or

(b) where the seller delivers a quantity of goods larger than he contracted to sell, reject the whole under subsection (2) above,

if the shortfall or, as the case may be, excess is so slight that it would be unreasonable for him to do so.

(2B) It is for the seller to show that a shortfall or excess fell within subsection (2A) above.

(2C) Subsections (2A) and (2B) above do not apply to Scotland.

(2D) Where the seller delivers a quantity of goods—

(a) less than he contracted to sell, the buyer shall not be entitled to reject the goods under subsection (1) above,

(b) larger than he contracted to sell, the buyer shall not be entitled to reject the whole under subsection (2) above,

unless the shortfall or excess is material.

(2E) Subsection (2D) above applies to Scotland only.

(3) Where the seller delivers to the buyer a quantity of goods larger than he contracted to sell and the buyer accepts the whole of the goods so delivered he must pay for them at the contract rate.

(4) [*Repealed.*]

(5) This section is subject to any usage of trade, special agreement, or course of dealing between the parties.

Instalment deliveries

31.—(1) Unless otherwise agreed, the buyer of goods is not bound to accept delivery of them by instalments.

(2) Where there is a contract for the sale of goods to be delivered by stated instalments, which are to be separately paid for, and the seller makes defective deliveries in respect of one or more instalments, or the buyer neglects or refuses to take delivery of or pay for one or more instalments, it is a question in each case depending on the terms of the contract and the circumstances of the case whether the breach of contract is a repudiation of the whole contract or whether it is a severable breach giving rise to a claim for compensation but not to a right to treat the whole contract as repudiated.

Delivery to carrier

32.—(1) Where, in pursuance of a contract of sale, the seller is authorised or required to send the goods to the buyer, delivery of the goods to a carrier (whether named by the buyer or not) for the purpose of transmission to the buyer is prima facie deemed to be a delivery of the goods to the buyer.

(2) Unless otherwise authorised by the buyer, the seller must make such contract with the carrier on behalf of the buyer as may be reasonable having regard to the nature of the goods and the other circumstances of the case; and if the seller omits to do so, and the goods are lost or damaged in course of transit, the buyer may decline to treat the delivery to the carrier as a delivery to himself or may hold the seller responsible in damages.

(3) Unless otherwise agreed, where goods are sent by the seller to the buyer by a route involving sea transit, under circumstances in which it is usual to insure, the seller must give such notice to the buyer as may enable him to insure them during their sea transit; and if the seller fails to do so, the goods are at his risk during such sea transit.

(4) In a case where the buyer deals as consumer or, in Scotland, where there is a consumer contract in which the buyer is a consumer, subsections (1) to (3) above must be ignored, but if in pursuance of a contract of sale the seller is authorised or required to send the goods to the buyer, delivery of the goods to the carrier is not delivery of the goods to the buyer.

Risk where goods are delivered at distant place

33. Where the seller of goods agrees to deliver them at his own risk at a place other than that where they are when sold, the buyer must nevertheless (unless otherwise agreed) take any risk of deterioration in the goods necessarily incident to the course of transit.

Buyer's right of examining the goods

34.—[*Subs. (1)—repealed*]
Unless otherwise agreed, when the seller tenders delivery of goods to the buyer, he is bound on request to afford the buyer a reasonable opportunity of examining the goods for the purpose of ascertaining whether they are in conformity with the contract and, in the case of a contract for sale by sample, of comparing the bulk with the sample.

Acceptance

35.—(1) The buyer is deemed to have accepted the goods
subject to subsection (2) below—

(a) when he intimates to the seller that he has accepted them, or

(b) when the goods have been delivered to him and he does any act in relation to them which is inconsistent with the ownership of the seller.

(2) Where goods are delivered to the buyer, and he has not previously examined them, he is not deemed to have accepted them under subsection

(1) above until he has had a reasonable opportunity of examining them for the purpose—

    (a) of ascertaining whether they are in conformity with the contract, and

    (b) in the case of a contract for sale by sample, of comparing the bulk with the sample.

(3) Where the buyer deals as consumer or (in Scotland) the contract of sale is a consumer contract, the buyer cannot lose his right to rely on subsection (2) above by agreement, waiver or otherwise.

(4) The buyer is also deemed to have accepted the goods when after the lapse of a reasonable time he retains the goods without intimating to the seller that he has rejected them.

(5) The questions that are material in determining for the purposes of subsection (4) above whether a reasonable time has elapsed include whether the buyer has had a reasonable opportunity of examining the goods for the purpose mentioned in subsection (2) above.

(6) The buyer is not by virtue of this section deemed to have accepted the goods merely because—

    (a) he asks for, or agrees to, their repair by or under an arrangement with the seller, or

    (b) the goods are delivered to another under a sub-sale or other disposition.

(7) Where the contract is for the sale of goods making one or more commercial units, a buyer accepting any goods included in a unit is deemed to have accepted all the goods making the unit; and in this subsection "commercial unit" means a unit division of which would materially impair the value of the goods or the character of the unit.

(8) Paragraph 10 of Schedule 1 below applies in relation to a contract made before 22 April 1967 or (in the application of this Act to Northern Ireland) 28 July 1967.

Right of partial rejection

    35A.—(1) If the buyer—

    (a) has the right to reject the goods by reason of a breach on the part of the seller that affects some or all of them, but

    (b) accepts some of the goods, including, where there are any goods unaffected by the breach, all such goods,

he does not by accepting them lose his right to reject the rest.

(2) in the case of a buyer having the right to reject an instalment of goods, subsection (1) above applies as if references to the goods were references to the goods comprised in the instalment.

(3) For the purposes of subsection (1) above, goods are affected by a breach if by reason of the breach they are not in conformity with the contract.

(4) This section applies unless a contrary intention appears in, or is to be implied from, the contract.

Buyer not bound to return rejected goods

36. Unless otherwise agreed, where goods are delivered to the buyer, and he refuses to accept them, having the right to do so, he is not bound to return them to the seller, but it is sufficient if he intimates to the seller that he refuses to accept them.

Buyer's liability for not taking delivery of goods

37.—(1) When the seller is ready and willing to deliver the goods, and requests the buyer to take delivery, and the buyer does not within a reasonable time after such request take delivery of the goods, he is liable to the seller for any loss occasioned by his neglect or refusal to take delivery, and also for a reasonable charge for the care and custody of the goods.

(2) Nothing in this section affects the rights of the seller where the neglect or refusal of the buyer to take delivery amounts to a repudiation of the contract.

PART V

RIGHTS OF UNPAID SELLER AGAINST THE GOODS

Preliminary

Unpaid seller defined

38.—(1) The seller of goods is an unpaid seller within the meaning of this Act—

(a) when the whole of the price has not been paid or tendered;

(b) when a bill of exchange or other negotiable instrument has been received as conditional payment, and the condition on which it was received has not been fulfilled by reason of the dishonour of the instrument or otherwise.

(2) In this Part of this Act "seller" includes any person who is in the position of a seller, as, for instance, an agent of the seller to whom the bill of lading has been indorsed, or a consignor or agent who has himself paid (or is directly responsible for) the price.

Unpaid seller's rights

39.—(1) Subject to this and any other Act, notwithstanding that the property in the goods may have passed to the buyer, the unpaid seller of goods, as such, has by implication of law—

(a) a lien on the goods or right to retain them for the price while he is in possession of them;

(b) in case of the insolvency of the buyer, a right of stopping the goods in transit after he has parted with the possession of them;

(c) a right of re-sale as limited by this Act.

(2) Where the property in goods has not passed to the buyer, the unpaid seller has (in addition to his other remedies) a right of withholding delivery similar to and co-extensive with his rights of lien or retention and stoppage in transit where the property has passed to the buyer.

Attachment by seller in Scotland

40. [*Repealed.*]

Unpaid Seller's Lien

Seller's lien

41.—(1) Subject to this Act, the unpaid seller of goods who is in possession of them is entitled to retain possession of them until payment or tender of the price in the following cases:—

(a) where the goods have been sold without any stipulation as to credit;

(b) where the goods have been sold on credit but the term of credit has expired;

(c) where the buyer becomes insolvent.

(2) The seller may exercise his lien or right of retention notwithstanding that he is in possession of the goods as agent or bailee or custodier for the buyer.

Part delivery

42. Where an unpaid seller has made part delivery of the goods, he may exercise his lien or right of retention on the remainder, unless such part delivery has been made under such circumstances as to show an agreement to waive the lien or right of retention.

Termination of lien

43.—(1) The unpaid seller of goods loses his lien or right of retention in respect of them—

(a) when he delivers the goods to a carrier or other bailee or custodier for the purpose of transmission to the buyer without reserving the right of disposal of the goods;

(b) when the buyer or his agent lawfully obtains possession of the goods;

(c) by waiver of the lien or right of retention.

(2) An unpaid seller of goods who has a lien or right of retention in respect of them does not lose his lien or right of retention by reason only that he has obtained judgment or decree for the price of the goods.

Stoppage in Transit

Right of stoppage in transit

44. Subject to this Act, when the buyer of goods becomes insolvent the unpaid seller who has parted with the possession of the goods has the right of stopping them in transit, that is to say, he may resume possession of the goods as long as they are in course of transit, and may retain them until payment or tender of the price.

Duration of transit

45.—(1) Goods are deemed to be in course of transit from the time when they are delivered to a carrier or other bailee or custodier for the purpose of transmission to the buyer, until the buyer or his agent in that behalf takes delivery of them from the carrier or other bailee or custodier.

(2) If the buyer or his agent in that behalf obtains delivery of the goods before their arrival at the appointed destination, the transit is at an end.

(3) If, after the arrival of the goods at the appointed destination, the carrier or other bailee or custodier acknowledges to the buyer or his agent that he holds the goods on his behalf and continues in possession of them as bailee or custodier for the buyer or his agent, the transit is at an end, and it is immaterial that a further destination for the goods may have been indicated by the buyer.

(4) If the goods are rejected by the buyer, and the carrier or other bailee or custodier continues in possession of them, the transit is not deemed to be at an end, even if the seller has refused to receive them back.

(5) When goods are delivered to a ship chartered by the buyer it is a question depending on the circumstances of the particular case whether they are in the possession of the master as a carrier or as agent to the buyer.

(6) Where the carrier or other bailee or custodier wrongfully refuses to deliver the goods to the buyer or his agent in that behalf, the transit is deemed to be at an end.

(7) Where part delivery of the goods has been made to the buyer or his agent in that behalf, the remainder of the goods may be stopped in transit, unless such part delivery has been made under such circumstances as to show an agreement to give up possession of the whole of the goods.

How stoppage in transit is effected

46.—(1) The unpaid seller may exercise his right of stoppage in transit either by taking actual possession of the goods or by giving notice of his claim to the carrier or other bailee or custodier in whose possession the goods are.

(2) The notice may be given either to the person in actual possession of the goods or to his principal.

(3) If given to the principal, the notice is ineffective unless given at such time and under such circumstances that the principal, by the exercise of reasonable diligence, may communicate it to his servant or agent in time to prevent a delivery to the buyer.

(4) When notice of stoppage in transit is given by the seller to the carrier or other bailee or custodier in possession of the goods, he must re-deliver the goods to, or according to the directions of, the seller; and the expenses of the re-delivery must be borne by the seller.

Re-sale, etc. by Buyer

Effect of sub-sale, etc. by buyer

47.—(1) Subject to this Act, the unpaid seller's right of lien or retention or stoppage in transit is not affected by any sale or other disposition of the goods which the buyer may have made, unless the seller has assented to it.

(2) Where a document of title to goods has been lawfully transferred to any person as buyer or owner of the goods, and that person transfers the document to a person who takes it in good faith and for valuable consideration, then—

(a) if the last-mentioned transfer was by way of sale the unpaid seller's right of lien or retention or stoppage in transit is defeated; and

(b) if the last-mentioned transfer was made by way of pledge or other disposition for value, the unpaid seller's right of lien or retention or stoppage in transit can only be exercised subject to the rights of the transferee.

Rescission: and Re-sale by Seller

Rescission: and re-sale by seller

48.—(1) Subject to this section, a contract of sale is not rescinded by the mere exercise by an unpaid seller of his right of lien or retention or stoppage in transit.

(2) Where an unpaid seller who has exercised his right of lien or retention or stoppage in transit re-sells the goods, the buyer acquires a good title to them as against the original buyer.

(3) Where the goods are of a perishable nature, or where the unpaid seller gives notice to the buyer of his intention to re-sell, and the buyer does not within a reasonable time pay or tender the price, the unpaid seller may re-sell the goods and recover from the original buyer damages for any loss occasioned by his breach of contract.

(4) Where the seller expressly reserves the right of re-sale in case the buyer should make default, and on the buyer making default re-sells the goods, the original contract of sale is rescinded but without prejudice to any claim the seller may have for damages.

PART 5A

ADDITIONAL RIGHTS OF BUYER IN CONSUMER CASES

48A Introductory

(1) This section applies if—

(a) the buyer deals as consumer or, in Scotland, there is a consumer contract in which the buyer is a consumer, and

(b) the goods do not conform to the contract of sale at the time of delivery.

(2) If this section applies, the buyer has the right—

(a) under and in accordance with section 48B below, to require the seller to repair or replace the goods, or

(b) under and in accordance with section 48C below—

    (i) to require the seller to reduce the purchase price of the goods to the buyer by an appropriate amount, or
    (ii) to rescind the contract with regard to the goods in question.

(3) For the purposes of subsection (1)(b) above goods which do not conform to the contract of sale at any time within the period of six months starting with the date on which the goods were delivered to the buyer must be taken not to have so conformed at that date.

(4) Subsection (3) above does not apply if—

(a) it is established that the goods did so conform at that date;

(b) its application is incompatible with the nature of the goods or the nature of the lack of conformity.

48B Repair or replacement of the goods

(1) If section 48A above applies, the buyer may require the seller—

(a) to repair the goods, or

(b) to replace the goods.

(2) If the buyer requires the seller to repair or replace the goods, the seller must—

(a) repair or, as the case may be, replace the goods within a reasonable time but without causing significant inconvenience to the buyer;

(b) bear any necessary costs incurred in doing so (including in particular the cost of any labour, materials or postage).

(3) The buyer must not require the seller to repair or, as the case may be, replace the goods if that remedy is—

(a) impossible or,

(b) disproportionate in comparison to the other of those remedies, or

(c) disproportionate in comparison to an appropriate reduction in the purchase price under paragraph (a), or rescission under paragraph (b), of section 48C(1) below.

(4) One remedy is disproportionate in comparison to the other if the one imposes costs on the seller which, in comparison to those imposed on him by the other, are unreasonable, taking into account—

(a) the value which the goods would have if they conformed to the contract of sale,

(b) the significance of the lack of conformity, and

(c) whether the other remedy could be effected without significant inconvenience to the buyer.

(5) Any question as to what is a reasonable time or significant inconvenience is to be determined by reference to—

(a) the nature of the goods, and

(b) the purpose for which the goods were acquired.

48C Reduction of purchase price or rescission of contract

(1) If section 48A above applies, the buyer may—

(a) require the seller to reduce the purchase price of the goods in question to the buyer by an appropriate amount, or

(b) rescind the contract with regard to those goods,

if the condition in subsection (2) below is satisfied.
(2) The condition is that—

(a) by virtue of section 48B(3) above the buyer may require neither repair nor replacement of the goods; or

(b) the buyer has required the seller to repair or replace the goods, but the seller is in breach of the requirement of section 48B(2)(a) above to do so within a reasonable time and without significant inconvenience to the buyer.

(3) For the purposes of this Part, if the buyer rescinds the contract, any reimbursement to the buyer may be reduced to take account of the use he has had of the goods since they were delivered to him.

48D Relation to other remedies etc.

(1) If the buyer requires the seller to repair or replace the goods the buyer must not act under subsection (2) until he has given the seller a reasonable time in which to repair or replace (as the case may be) the goods.

(2) The buyer acts under this subsection if—

  (a) in England and Wales or Northern Ireland he rejects the goods and terminates the contract for breach of condition;

  (b) in Scotland he rejects any goods delivered under the contract and treats it as repudiated;

  (c) he requires the goods to be replaced or repaired (as the case may be).

48E Powers of the court

(1) In any proceedings in which a remedy is sought by virtue of this Part the court, in addition to any other power it has, may act under this section.

(2) On the application of the buyer the court may make an order requiring specific performance or, in Scotland, specific implement by the seller of any obligation imposed on him by virtue of section 48B above.

(3) Subsection (4) applies if—

  (a) the buyer requires the seller to give effect to a remedy under section 48B or 48C above or has claims to rescind under section 48C, but

  (b) the court decides that another remedy under section 48B or 48C is appropriate.

(4) The court may proceed—

  (a) as if the buyer had required the seller to give effect to the other remedy, or if the other remedy is rescission under section 48C

  (b) as if the buyer had claimed to rescind the contract under that section.

(5) If the buyer has claimed to rescind the contract the court may order that any reimbursement to the buyer is reduced to take account of the use he has had of the goods since they were delivered to him.

(6) The court may make an order under this section unconditionally or on such terms and conditions as to damages, payment of the price and otherwise as it thinks just.

48F Conformity with the contract

For the purposes of this Part, goods do not conform to a contract of sale if there is, in relation to the goods, a breach of an express term of the contract or a term implied by section 13, 14 or 15 above.

PART VI

ACTIONS FOR BREACH OF THE CONTRACT

Seller's Remedies

Action for price

49.—(1) Where, under a contract of sale, the property in the goods has passed to the buyer and he wrongfully neglects or refuses to pay for the goods according to the terms of the contract, the seller may maintain an action against him for the price of the goods.

(2) Where, under a contract of sale, the price is payable on a day certain irrespective of delivery and the buyer wrongfully neglects or refuses to pay such price, the seller may maintain an action for the price, although the property in the goods has not passed and the goods have not been appropriated to the contract.

(3) Nothing in this section prejudices the right of the seller in Scotland to recover interest on the price from the date of tender of the goods, or from the date on which the price was payable, as the case may be.

Damages for non-acceptance

50.—(1) Where the buyer wrongfully neglects or refuses to accept and pay for the goods, the seller may maintain an action against him for damages for non-acceptance.

(2) The measure of damages is the estimated loss directly and naturally resulting, in the ordinary course of events, from the buyer's breach of contract.

(3) Where there is an available market for the goods in question the measure of damages is prima facie to be ascertained by the difference between the contract price and the market or current price at the time or times when the goods ought to have been accepted or (if no time was fixed for acceptance) at the time of the refusal to accept.

Buyer's Remedies

Damages for non-delivery

51.—(1) Where the seller wrongfully neglects or refuses to deliver the goods to the buyer, the buyer may maintain an action against the seller for damages for non-delivery.

(2) The measure of damages is the estimated loss directly and naturally resulting, in the ordinary course of events, from the seller's breach of contract.

(3) Where there is an available market for the goods in question the measure of damages is prima facie to be ascertained by the difference between the contract price and the market or current price of the goods at the time or times when they ought to have been delivered or (if no time was fixed) at the time of the refusal to deliver.

Specific performance

52.—(1) In any action for breach of contract to deliver specific or ascertained goods the court may, if it thinks fit, on the plaintiff's application, by its judgment or decree direct that the contract shall be performed specifically, without giving the defendant the option of retaining the goods on payment of damages.

(2) The plaintiff's application may be made at any time before judgment or decree.

(3) The judgment or decree may be unconditional, or on such terms and conditions as to damages, payment of the price and otherwise as seem just to the court.

(4) The provisions of this section shall be deemed to be supplementary to, and not in derogation of, the right of specific implement in Scotland.

Remedy for breach of warranty

53.—(1) Where there is a breach of warranty by the seller, or where the buyer elects (or is compelled) to treat any breach of a condition on the part of the seller as a breach of warranty, the buyer is not by reason only of such breach of warranty entitled to reject the goods; but he may—

(a) set up against the seller the breach of warranty in diminution or extinction of the price, or

(b) maintain an action against the seller for damages for the breach of warranty.

(2) The measure of damages for breach of warranty is the estimated loss directly and naturally resulting, in the ordinary course of events, from the breach of warranty.

(3) In the case of breach of warranty of quality such loss is prima facie the difference between the value of the goods at the time of delivery to the buyer and the value they would have had if they had fulfilled the warranty.

(4) The fact that the buyer has set up the breach of warranty in diminution or extinction of the price does not prevent him from maintaining an action for the same breach of warranty if he has suffered further damage.

(5) This section does not apply to Scotland.

Measure of damages as respects Scotland

53A.—(1) The measure of damages for the seller's breach of contract is the estimated loss directly and naturally resulting, in the ordinary course of events, from the breach.

(2) Where the seller's breach consists of the delivery of goods which are not of the quality required by the contract and the buyer retains the goods, such loss as aforesaid is prima facie the difference between the value of the goods at the time of delivery to the buyer and the value they would have had if they had fulfilled the contract.

(3) This section applies to Scotland only.

Interest, etc.

54. Nothing in this Act affects the right of the buyer or the seller to recover interest or special damages in any case where by law interest or special damages may be recoverable, or to recover money paid where the consideration for the payment of it has failed.

PART VII

SUPPLEMENTARY

Exclusion of implied terms

55.—(1) Where a right, duty or liability would arise under a contract of sale of goods by implication of law, it may (subject to the Unfair Contract Terms Act 1977) be ncgatived or varied by express agreement, or by the course of dealing between the parties, or by such usage as binds both parties to the contract.

(2) An express term does not negative a term implied by this Act unless inconsistent with it.

(3) Paragraph 11 of Schedule 1 below applies in relation to a contract made on or after 18 May 1973 and before 1 February 1978, and paragraph 12 in relation to one made before 18 May 1973.

Conflict of laws

56. Paragraph 13 of Schedule 1 below applies in relation to a contract made on or after 18 May 1973 and before 1 February 1978, so as to make provision about conflict of laws in relation to such a contract.

Auction sales

57.—(1) Where goods are put up for sale by auction in lots, each lot is *prima facie* deemed to be the subject of a separate contract of sale.

(2) A sale by auction is complete when the auctioneer announces its completion by the fall of the hammer, or in other customary manner; and until the announcement is made any bidder may retract his bid.

(3) A sale by auction may be notified to be subject to a reserve or upset price, and a right to bid may also be reserved expressly by or on behalf of the seller.

(4) Where a sale by auction is not notified to be subject to a right to bid by or on behalf of the seller, it is not lawful for the seller to bid himself or to employ any person to bid at the sale, or for the auctioneer knowingly to take any bid from the seller or any such person.

(5) A sale contravening subsection (4) above may be treated as fraudulent by the buyer.

(6) Where, in respect of a sale by auction, a right to bid is expressly reserved (but not otherwise) the seller or any one person on his behalf may bid at the auction.

Payment into court in Scotland

58. In Scotland where a buyer has elected to accept goods which he might have rejected, and to treat a breach of contract as only giving rise to a claim for damages, he may, in an action by the seller for the price, be required, in the discretion of the court before which the action depends, to consign or pay into court the price of the goods, or part of the price, or to give other reasonable security for its due payment.

Reasonable time a question of fact

59. Where a reference is made in this Act to a reasonable time the question what is a reasonable time is a question of fact.

Rights, etc. enforceable by action

60. Where a right, duty or liability is declared by this Act, it may (unless otherwise provided by this Act) be enforced by action.

Interpretation

61.—(1) In this Act, unless the context or subject matter otherwise requires,—

"action" includes counterclaim and set-off, and in Scotland condescendence and claim and compensation;

"bulk" means a mass or collection of goods of the same kind which—

(a) is contained in a defined space or area; and
(b) is such that any goods in the bulk are interchangeable with any other goods therein of the same number or quantity;

"business" includes a profession and the activities of any government department (including a Northern Ireland department) or local or public authority;

"buyer" means a person who buys or agrees to buy goods;

"consumer contract" has the same meaning as in section 25(1) of the Unfair Contract Terms Act 1977; and for the purposes of this Act the onus of proving that a contract is not to be regarded as a consumer contract shall lie on the seller;

"contract of sale" includes an agreement to sell as well as a sale;

"credit-broker" means a person acting in the course of a business of credit brokerage carried on by him, that is a business of effecting introductions of individuals desiring to obtain credit—

(a) to persons carrying on any business so far as it relates to the provision of credit, or
(b) to other persons engaged in credit brokerage;

"defendant" includes in Scotland defender, respondent, and claimant in a multiplepoinding;

"delivery" means voluntary transfer of possession from one person to another except that in relation to sections 20A and 20B above it includes such appropriation of goods to the contract as results in property in the goods being transferred to the buyer.

"document of title to goods" has the same meaning as it has in the Factors Acts;

"Factors Acts" means the Factors Act 1889, the Factors (Scotland) Act 1890, and any enactment amending or substituted for the same;

"fault" means wrongful act or default;

"future goods" means goods to be manufactured or acquired by the seller after the making of the contract of sale;

"goods" includes all personal chattels other than things in action and money, and in Scotland all corporeal moveables except money; and in particular "goods" includes emblements, industrial growing crops, and things attached to or forming part of the land which are agreed to be severed before sale or under the contract of sale and includes an undivided share in goods;

"plaintiff " includes pursuer, complainer, claimant in a multiplepoinding and defendant or defender counter-claiming;

"producer" means the manufacturer of goods, the importer of goods into the European Economic Area or any person purporting to be a producer by placing his name, trade mark or other distinctive sign on the goods;

"property" means the general property in goods, and not merely a special property;

["*quality*"—*repealed*;]

[135]

"repair" means, in cases where there is a lack of conformity in goods for the purposes of section 48F of this Act, to bring the goods into conformity with the contract;

"sale" includes a bargain and sale as well as a sale and delivery;

"seller" means a person who sells or agrees to sell goods;

"specific goods" means goods identified and agreed on at the time a contract of sale is made and includes an undivided share, specified as a fraction or percentage, of goods identified and agreed on as aforesaid;

"warranty" (as regards England and Wales and Northern Ireland) means an agreement with reference to goods which are the subject of a contract of sale, but collateral to the main purpose of such contract, the breach of which gives rise to a claim for damages, but not to a right to reject the goods and treat the contract as repudiated.

(2) [*Repealed.*]

(3) A thing is deemed to be done in good faith within the meaning of this Act when it is in fact done honestly, whether it is done negligently or not.

(4) A person is deemed to be insolvent within the meaning of this Act if he has either ceased to pay his debts in the ordinary course of business or he cannot pay his debts as they become due, [...]

(5) Goods are in a deliverable state within the meaning of this Act when they are in such a state that the buyer would under the contract be bound to take delivery of them.

(5A) References in this Act to dealing as consumer are to be construed in accordance with Part I of the Unfair Contract Terms Act 1977; and, for the purposes of this Act, it is for a seller claiming that the buyer does not deal as consumer to show that he does not.

(6) As regards the definition of "business" in subsection (1) above, paragraph 14 of Schedule 1 below applies in relation to a contract made on or after 18 May 1973 and before 1 February 1978, and paragraph 15 in relation to one made before 18 May 1973.

Savings: rules of law, etc.

62.—(1) The rules in bankruptcy relating to contracts of sale apply to those contracts, notwithstanding anything in this Act.

(2) The rules of the common law, including the law merchant, except in so far as they are inconsistent with the provisions of this Act, and in particular the rules relating to the law of principal and agent and the effect of fraud, misrepresentation, duress or coercion, mistake, or other invalidating cause, apply to contracts for the sale of goods.

(3) Nothing in this Act or the Sale of Goods Act 1893 affects the enactments relating to bills of sale, or any enactment relating to the sale of goods which is not expressly repealed or amended by this Act or that.

(4) The provisions of this Act about contracts of sale do not apply to a transaction in the form of a contract of sale which is intended to operate by way of mortgage, pledge, charge, or other security.

(5) Nothing in this Act prejudices or affects the landlord's right of hypothec or sequestration for rent in Scotland.

Consequential amendments, repeals and savings

63.—(1) Without prejudice to section 17 of the Interpretation Act 1978 (repeal and re-enactment), the enactments mentioned in Schedule 2 below have effect subject to the amendments there specified (being amendments consequential on this Act).

(2) The enactments mentioned in Schedule 3 below are repealed to the extent specified in column 3, but subject to the savings in Schedule 4 below.

(3) The savings in Schedule 4 below have effect.

Short title and commencement

64.—(1) This Act may be cited as the Sale of Goods Act 1979.

(2) This Act comes into force on 1 January 1980.

SCHEDULES 1 to 4—see *Benjamin*, pp.1962–1972.

APPENDIX B

DIRECTIVE 1999/44/EC OF THE EUROPEAN PARLIAMENT AND OF THE COUNCIL of 25 May 1999
on certain aspects of the sale of consumer goods and associated guarantees

THE EUROPEAN PARLIAMENT AND THE COUNCIL OF THE EUROPEAN UNION,

Having regard to the Treaty establishing the European Community, and in particular Article 95 thereof,

B–001

Having regard to the proposal from the Commission,[1]

Having regard to the opinion of the Economic and Social Committee,[2]

Acting in accordance with the procedure laid down in Article 251 of the Treaty in the light of the joint text approved by the Conciliation Committee on 18 May 1999,[3]

(1) Whereas Article 153(1) and (3) of the Treaty provides that the Community should contribute to the achievement of a high level of consumer protection by the measures it adopts pursuant to Article 95 thereof;

(2) Whereas the internal market comprises an area without internal frontiers in which the free movement of goods, persons, services and capital is guaranteed; whereas free movement of goods concerns not only transactions by persons acting in the course of a business but also transactions by private individuals; whereas it implies that consumers resident in one Member State should be free to purchase goods in the territory of another Member State on the basis of a uniform minimum set of fair rules governing the sale of consumer goods;

(3) Whereas the laws of the Member States concerning the sale of consumer goods are somewhat disparate, with the result that national

---

[1] O.J. C307/8 and O.J. C148/12.
[2] O.J. C66/5.
[3] Opinion of the European Parliament of 10 March, 1998 (O.J. C104/30), Council Common Position of 24 September, 1998 (O.J. C333/46) and Decision of the European Parliament of 17 December, 1998 (O.J. C98/226). Decision of the European Parliament of 5 May, 1999. Council Decision of 17 May, 1999.

consumer goods markets differ from one another and that competition between sellers may be distorted;

(4) Whereas consumers who are keen to benefit from the large market by purchasing goods in Member States other than their State of residence play a fundamental role in the completion of the internal market; whereas the artificial reconstruction of frontiers and the compartmentalisation of markets should be prevented; whereas the opportunities available to consumers have been greatly broadened by new communication technologies which allow ready access to distribution systems in other Member States or in third countries; whereas, in the absence of minimum harmonisation of the rules governing the sale of consumer goods, the development of the sale of goods through the medium of new distance communication technologies risks being impeded;

(5) Whereas the creation of a common set of minimum rules of consumer law, valid no matter where goods are purchased within the Community, will strengthen consumer confidence and enable consumers to make the most of the internal market;

(6) Whereas the main difficulties encountered by consumers and the main source of disputes with sellers concern the non-conformity of goods with the contract; whereas it is therefore appropriate to approximate national legislation governing the sale of consumer goods in this respect, without however impinging on provisions and principles of national law relating to contractual and non-contractual liability;

(7) Whereas the goods must, above all, conform with the contractual specifications; whereas the principle of conformity with the contract may be considered as common to the different national legal traditions; whereas in certain national legal traditions it may not be possible to rely solely on this principle to ensure a minimum level of protection for the consumer; whereas under such legal traditions, in particular, additional national provisions may be useful to ensure that the consumer is protected in cases where the parties have agreed no specific contractual terms or where the parties have concluded contractual terms or agreements which directly or indirectly waive or restrict the rights of the consumer and which, to the extent that these rights result from this Directive, are not binding on the consumer;

(8) Whereas, in order to facilitate the application of the principle of conformity with the contract, it is useful to introduce a rebuttable presumption of conformity with the contract covering the most common situations; whereas that presumption does not restrict the principle of freedom of contract; whereas, furthermore, in the absence of specific contractual terms, as well as where the minimum protection clause is applied, the elements mentioned in this presumption may be used to determine the lack of conformity of the goods with the contract;

whereas the quality and performance which consumers can reasonably expect will depend *inter alia* on whether the goods are new or second-hand; whereas the elements mentioned in the presumption are cumulative; whereas, if the circumstances of the case render any particular element manifestly inappropriate, the remaining elements of the presumption nevertheless still apply;

(9) Whereas the seller should be directly liable to the consumer for the conformity of the goods with the contract; whereas this is the traditional solution enshrined in the legal orders of the Member States; whereas nevertheless the seller should be free, as provided for by national law, to pursue remedies against the producer, a previous seller in the same chain of contracts or any other intermediary, unless he has remounced that entitlement; whereas this Directive does not affect the principle of freedom of contract between the seller, the producer, a previous seller or any other intermediary; whereas the rules governing against whom and how the seller may pursue such remedies are to be determined by national law;

(10) Whereas, in the case of non-conformity of the goods with the contract, consumers should be entitled to have the goods restored to conformity with the contract free of charge, choosing either repair or replacement, or, failing this, to have the price reduced or the contract rescinded;

(11) Whereas the consumer in the first place may require the seller to repair the goods or to replace them unless those remedies are impossible or disproportionate; whereas whether a remedy is disproportionate should be determined objectively; whereas a remedy would be disproportionate if it imposed, in comparison with the other remedy, unreasonable costs; whereas, in order to determine whether the costs are unreasonable, the costs of one remedy should be significantly higher than the costs of the other remedy;

(12) Whereas in cases of a lack of conformity, the seller may always offer the consumer, by way of settlement, any available remedy; whereas it is for the consumer to decide whether to accept or reject this proposal;

(13) Whereas, in order to enable consumers to take advantage of the internal market and to buy consumer goods in another Member State, it should be recommended that, in the interests of consumers, the producers of consumer goods that are marketed in several Member States attach to the product a list with at least one contact address in every Member State where the product is marketed;

(14) Whereas the references to the time of delivery do not imply that Member States have to change their rules on the passing of the risk;

(15) Whereas Member States may provide that any reimbursement to the consumer may be reduced to take account of the use the consumer has had of the goods since they were delivered to him; whereas the

detailed arrangements whereby rescission of the contract is effected may be laid down in national law;

(16) Whereas the specific nature of second-hand goods makes it generally impossible to replace them; whereas therefore the consumer's right of replacement is generally not available for these goods; whereas for such goods, Member States may enable the parties to agree a short-ened period of liability;

(17) Whereas it is appropriate to limit in time the period during which the seller is liable for any lack of conformity which exists at the time of delivery of the goods; whereas Member States may also provide for a limitation on the period during which consumers can exercise their rights, provided such a period does not expire within two years from the time of delivery; whereas where, under national legislation, the time when a limitation period starts is not the time of delivery of the goods, the total duration of the limitation period provided for by national law may not be shorter than two years from the time of delivery;

(18) Whereas Member States may provide for suspension or interruption of the period during which any lack of conformity must become apparent and of the limitation period, where applicable and in accord-ance with their national law, in the event of repair, replacement or negotiations between seller and consumer with a view to an amicable settlement;

(19) Whereas Member States should be allowed to set a period within which the consumer must inform the seller of any lack of conformity; whereas Member States may ensure a higher level of protection for the consumer by not introducing such an obligation; whereas in any case consumers throughout the Community should have at least two months in which to inform the seller that a lack of conformity exists;

(20) Whereas Member States should guard against such a period placing at a disadvantage consumers shopping across borders; whereas all Mem-ber States should inform the Commission of their use of this pro-vision; whereas the Commission should monitor the effect of the varied application of this provision on consumers and on the internal market; whereas information on the use made of this provision by a Member State should be available to the other Member States and to consumers and consumer organisations throughout the Community; whereas a summary of the situation in all Member States should therefore be published in the *Official Journal of the European Communities*;

(21) Whereas, for certain categories of goods, it is current practice for sell-ers and producers to offer guarantees on goods against any defect which becmes apparent within a certain period; whereas this practice can stimulate competition; whereas, while such guarantees are legit-imate marketing tools, they should not mislead the consumer;

whereas, to ensure that consumers are not misled, guarantees should contain certain information, including a statement that the guarantee does not affect the consumer's legal rights;

(22) Whereas the parties may not, by common consent, restrict or waive the rights granted to consumers, since otherwise the legal protection afforded would be thwarted; whereas this principle should apply also to clauses which imply that the consumer was aware of any lack of conformity of the consumer goods existing at the time the contract was concluded; whereas the protection granted to consumers under this Directive should not be reduced on the grounds that the law of a non-member State has been chosen as being applicable to the contract;

(23) Whereas legislation and case-law in this area in the various Member States show that there is growing concern to ensure a high level of consumer protection; whereas, in the light of this trend and the experience acquired in implementing this Directive, it may be necessary to envisage more far-reaching harmonisation, notably by providing for the producer's direct liability for defects for which he is responsible;

(24) Whereas Member States should be allowed to adopt or maintain in force more stringent provisions in the field covered by this Directive to ensure an even higher level of consumer protection;

(25) Whereas, according to the Commission recommendation of 30 March 1998 on the principles applicable to the bodies responsible for out-of-court settlement of consumer disputes[4], Member States can create bodies that ensure impartial and efficient handling of complaints in a national and cross-border context and which consumers can use as mediators;

(26) Whereas it is appropriate, in order to protect the collective interests of consumers, to add this Directive to the list of Directives contained in the Annex to Directive 98/27/EC of the European Parliament and of the Council of 19 May 1998 on injunctions for the protection of consumers' interests[5],

HAVE ADOPTED THIS DIRECTIVE:

Article 1

Scope and definitions

1. The purpose of this Directive is the approximation of the laws, regulations and administrative provisions of the Member States on certain

---

[4] O.J. L115/31.
[5] O.J. L166/51.

aspects of the sale of consumer goods and associated guarantees in order to ensure a uniform minimum level of consumer protection in the context of the internal market.

2. For the purposes of this Directive:

(a) *consumer*: shall mean any natural person who, in the contracts covered by this Directive, is acting for purposes which are not related to his trade, business or profession;

(b) *consumer goods*: shall mean any tangible movable item, with the exception of:

— goods sold by way of execution or otherwise by authority of law,
— water and gas where they are not put up for sale in a limited volume or set quantity,
— electricity;

(c) *seller*: shall mean any natural or legal person who, under a contract, sells consumer goods in the course of his trade, business or profession;

(d) *producer*: shall mean the manufacturer of consumer goods, the importer of consumer goods into the territory of the Community or any person purporting to be a producer by placing his name, trade mark or other distinctive sign on the consumer goods;

(e) *guarantee*: shall mean any undertaking by a seller or producer to the consumer, given without extra charge, to reimburse the price paid or to replace, repair or handle consumer goods in any way if they do not meet the specifications set out in the guarantee statement or in the relevant advertising;

(f) *repair*: shall mean, in the event of lack of conformity, bringing consumer goods into conformity with the contract of sale.

3. Member States may provide that the expression 'consumer goods' does not cover second-hand goods sold at public auction where consumers have the opportunity of attending the sale in person.

4. Contracts for the supply of consumer goods to be manufactured or produced shall also be deemed contracts of sale for the purpose of this Directive.

Article 2

Conformity with the contract

1. The seller must deliver goods to the consumer which are in conformity with the contract of sale.

2. Consumer goods are presumed to be in conformity with the contract if they:

(a) comply with the description given by the seller and possess the qualities of the goods which the seller has held out to the consumer as a sample or model;

(b) are fit for any particular purpose for which the consumer requires them and which he made known to the seller at the time of conclusion of the contract and which the seller has accepted;

(c) are fit for the purposes for which goods of the same type are normally used;

(d) show the quality and performance which are normal in goods of the same type and which the consumer can reasonably expect, given the nature of the goods and taking into account any public statements on the specific characteristics of the goods made about them by the seller, the producer or his representative, particularly in advertising or on labelling.

3. There shall be deemed not to be a lack of conformity for the purposes of this Article if, at the time the contract was concluded, the consumer was aware, or could not reasonably be unaware of, the lack of conformity, or if the lack of conformity has its origin in materials supplied by the consumer.

4. The seller shall not be bound by public statements, as referred to in paragraph 2(d) if he:

— shows that he was not, and could not reasonably have been, aware of the statement in question,

— shows that by the time of conclusion of the contract the statement had been corrected, or

— shows that the decision to buy the consumer goods could not have been influenced by the statement.

5. Any lack of conformity resulting from incorrect installation of the consumer goods shall be deemed to be equivalent to lack of conformity of the goods if installation forms part of the contract of sale of the goods and the goods were installed by the seller or under his responsibility. This shall apply equally if the product, intended to be installed by the consumer, is installed by the consumer and the incorrect installation is due to a shortcoming in the installation instructions.

Article 3

Rights of the consumer

1. The seller shall be liable to the consumer for any lack of conformity which exists at the time the goods were delivered.

2. In the case of a lack of conformity, the consumer shall be entitled to have the goods brought into conformity free of charge by repair or replacement, in accordance with paragraph 3, or to have an appropriate reduction made in the price or the contract rescinded with regard to those goods, in accordance with paragraphs 5 and 6.

3. In the first place, the consumer may require the seller to repair the goods or he may require the seller to replace them, in either case free of charge, unless this is impossible or disproportionate.

A remedy shall be deemd to be disproportionate if it imposes costs on the seller which, in comparison with the alternative remedy, are unreasonable, taking into account:

— the value the goods would have if there were no lack of conformity,

— the significance of the lack of conformity, and

— whether the alternative remedy could be completed without significant inconvenience to the consumer.

Any repair or replacement shall be completed within a reasonable time and without any significant inconvenience to the consumer, taking account of the nature of the goods and the purpose for which the consumer required the goods.

4. The terms 'free of charge' in paragraphs 2 and 3 refer to the necessary costs incurred to bring the goods into conformity, particularly the cost of postage, labour and materials.

5. The consumer may require an appropriate reduction of the price or have the contract rescinded:

— if the consumer is entitled to neither repair nor replacement, or

— if the seller has not completed the remedy within a reasonable time, or

— if the seller has not completed the remedy without significant inconvenience to the consumer.

6. The consumer is not entitled to have the contract rescinded if the lack of conformity is minor.

Article 4

Right of redress

Where the final seller is liable to the consumer because of a lack of conformity resulting from an act or omission by the producer, a previous seller in the same chain of contracts or any other intermediary, the final seller shall be entitled to pursue remedies against the person or persons liable in the contractual chain. The person or persons liable against whom the final seller may pursue remedies, together with the relevant actions and conditions of exercise, shall be determined by national law.

Article 5

Time limits

1. The seller shall be held liable under Article 3 where the lack of conformity becomes apparent within two years as from delivery of the goods. If, under national legislation, the rights laid down in Article 3(2) are subject to a limitation period, that period shall not expire within a period of two years from the time of delivery.

2. Member States may provide that, in order to benefit from his rights, the consumer must inform the seller of the lack of conformity within a period of two months from the date on which he detected such lack of conformity.

Member States shall inform the Commission of their use of this paragraph. The Commission shall monitor the effect of the existence of this option for the Member States on consumers and on the internal market.

Not later than 7 January 2003, the Commission shall prepare a report on the use made by Member States of this paragraph. This report shall be published in the *Official Journal of the European Communities*.

3. Unless proved otherwise, any lack of conformity which becomes apparent within six months of delivery of the goods shall be presumed to have existed at the time of delivery unless this presumption is incompatible with the nature of the goods or the nature of the lack of conformity.

Article 6

Guarantees

1. A guarantee shall be legally binding on the offerer under the conditions laid down in the guarantee statement and the associated advertising.

2. The guarantee shall:

— state that the consumer has legal rights under applicable national legislation governing the sale of consumer goods and make clear that those rights are not affected by the guarantee,

    — set out in plain intelligible language the contents of the guarantee and the essential particulars necessary for making claims under the guarantee, notably the duration and territorial scope of the guarantee as well as the name and address of the guarantor.

3. On request by the consumer, the guarantee shall be made available in writing or feature in another durable medium available and accessible to him.

4. Within its own territory, the Member State in which the consumer goods are marketed may, in accordance with the rules of the Treaty, provide that the guarantee be drafted in one or more languages which it shall determine from among the official languages of the Community.

5. Should a guarantee infringe the requirements of paragraphs 2, 3 or 4, the validity of this guarantee shall in no way be affected, and the consumer can still rely on the guarantee and require that it be honoured.

Article 7

Binding nature

1. Any contractual terms or agreements concluded with the seller before the lack of conformity is brought to the seller's attention which directly or indirectly waive or restrict the rights resulting from this Directive shall, as provided for by national law, not be binding on the consumer.

Member States may provide that, in the case of second-hand goods, the seller and consumer may agree contractual terms or agreements which have a shorter time period for the liability of the seller than that set down in Article 5(1). Such period may not be less than one year.

2. Member States shall take the necessary measures to ensure that consumers are not deprived on the protection afforded by this Directive as a result of opting for the law of a non-member State as the law applicable to the contract where the contract has a close connection with the territory of the Member States.

Article 8

National law and minimum protection

1. The rights resulting from this Directive shall be exercised without prejudice to other rights which the consumer may invoke under the national rules governing contractual or non-contractual liability.

2. Member States may adopt or maintain in force more stringent provisions, compatible with the Treaty in the field covered by this Directive, to ensure a higher level of consumer protection.

Article 9

Member States shall take appropriate measures to inform the consumer of the national law transposing this Directive and shall encourage, where appropriate, professional organisations to inform consumers of their rights.

Article 10

The Annex to Directive 98/27/EC shall be completed as follows:

'10. Directive 1999/44/EC of the European Parliament and of the Council of 25 May 1999 on certain aspects of the sale of consumer goods and associated guarantees (O.J. L171, 7.7.1999, p.12).'

Article 11

Transposition

1. Member States shall bring into force the laws, regulations and administrative provisions necessary to comply with this Directive not later than 1 January 2002. They shall forthwith inform the Commission thereof.

When Member States adopt these measures, they shall contain a reference to this Directive, or shall be accompanied by such reference at the time of their official publication. The procedure for such reference shall be adopted by Member States.

2. Member States shall communicate to the Commission the provisions of national law which they adopt in the field covered by this Directive.

Article 12

Review

The Commission shall, not later than 7 July 2006, review the application of this Directive and submit to the European Parliament and the Council a report. The report shall examine, *inter alia*, the case for introducing the producer's direct liability and, if appropriate, shall be accompanied by proposals.

Article 13

Entry into force

This Directive shall enter into force on the day of its publication in the *Official Journal of the European Communities*.

Article 14

This Directive is addressed to the Member States.

Done at Brussels, 25 May 1999.

For the European Parliament	*For the Council*
The President	*The President*
J.M. GIL-ROBLES	H.EICHEL

INDEX

[151]